T.O.H.P. Burnham

Home songs for little darlings

T.O.H.P. Burnham

Home songs for little darlings

ISBN/EAN: 9783744768115

Printed in Europe, USA, Canada, Australia, Japan

Cover: Foto ©Thomas Meinert / pixelio.de

More available books at **www.hansebooks.com**

"In books, or work, or healthful play,
Let my first years be passed ;
That I may give for every day
Some good account at last."

Home Songs

FOR

LITTLE DARLINGS.

As years make us wiser or prouder,
What innocent pleasures we miss;
The rattles of life may be louder,
But are not so harmless as this.

BOSTON:

T. O. H. P. BURNHAM,

143 WASHINGTON STREET.

1863.

RIVERSIDE, CAMBRIDGE: PRINTED BY H. O. HOUGHTON.

Home Songs for Little Darlings.

WILLIE'S BIRTHDAY.

THOU wakest from rosy sleep to play
    With bounding heart, my boy!
Beyond thee lies a long bright day
    Of summer and of joy.

Thou hast no heavy thought or dream
    To cloud thy fearless eye;
Long be it thus — life's early stream
    Should still reflect the sky.

(7)

Let ere the cares of life lie dim
  On thy young spirit's wings,
Now in thy morn forget not him
  From whom each pure thought springs:

So in the onward vale of tears,
  Where'er thy path may be,
When strength hath bowed to evil years,
  He will remember thee.
                                    Hemans.

———◆———

MORNING PRAYER.

GREAT God, who dwells in heaven above,
  I humbly kneel to thee,
To thank thee for the care and love
  Which thou dost show to me.

When in the early morn I rise
  To see another day,
From thy commands so good and wise,
  Let not my footsteps stray.

And bless my parents, good and dear,
  Teach me to grateful be,
For all the kind and watchful care
  They lavish upon me.

Oh, keep my feet in virtue's paths,
    As through this world I move,
That I at last may sit with thee,
    In thy bright realms above.

ROBIN REDBREAST.

WHEN the fields are white with snow,
And the frosty breezes blow,
Pretty Robin Redbreast comes,
Watching for the children's crumbs.

Crimson breast and diamond eye,
In he hops, both bold and shy;
With a timid, gentle glance,
Eyes the children all askance.

Pretty Robin, dread no harm!
Start not off in vain alarm!
See, he pecks the crumbs so sweet,
Grateful for the warm retreat.

Who has never dropt a tear
O'er the tale of children dear,
In the wood who dying lay,
Led by cruel men astray;

And how Robin Redbreast there
Spread with leaves the hapless pair! —
Hence each young and tender breast
Loves of birds the Robin best.

———◆———

THE PONY RIDE.

PRETTY lady, mount and go!
    Saddle, bridle, all is ready,
And the pony's glances show,
    He is proud to bear his lady.

Cæsar barks with honest glee,
    All impatient for a scamper;
Down the road or o'er the lea
    Off he 'll bound before the tramper.

Trot or amble, safe and sure,
    Pony ne'er will start or stumble;
Over holt or hill secure,
    Mount and go, nor fear a tumble.

Pony well deserves your care,
    Corn and hay to fill his manger;
Well he knows his mistress fair,
    Knows her voice from any stranger.

MY LITTLE SISTER.

O MOTHER, look at baby,
    See how she jumps and crows;
That 't is her little sister
    I really think she knows.

And do you think she loves me
    And wants me by her side,
To gather up her playthings,
    And teach her how to ride,

And place her in her cradle
  When she wants to go to sleep,
To rock it softly when she stirs,
  And by its side to keep?

I'm sure I love her dearly,
  And hope that she will me,
When she comes to know more clearly
  How dear she is to me.

And every night to God I'll pray,
  On his bright throne above,
To make me dear to baby,
  And worthy of her love.

—◆—

THE CHORUS OF FROGS.

"YAUP, yaup, yaup,"
Said the croaking voice of a Frog:
  "A rainy day,
  In the month of May,
And plenty of room in the bog."

"Yaup, yaup, yaup,"
Said the Frog, as he hopped away:
  "The insects feed
  On the floating weed,
And I'm hungry for dinner to-day."

"Yaup, yaup, yaup,"
Said the Frog, as it splashed about :
  " Good neighbors all,
    When you hear me call,
It is odd that you do not come out."

" Yaup, yaup, yaup,"
Said the frogs; " it is charming weather,
    We'll come and sup
    When the moon is up,
And we 'll all of us croak together."

———•———

THE RECONCILEMENT.

Two brothers once fell out at play,
    As little boys will do,
Whose parents reconciled the fray
    By gentle means and true.

No threats severe they vainly try,
    No angry word or blow,
But kind entreaties thus apply,
    From loving lips that flow : —

" Dear children, join your hands in love,
    And he that first shall smile,

A noble boy himself will prove,   .
   Above revenge or guile.

" And oh! while blest with life and light,
   Let not the sun go down
On angry breasts that brawl and fight,
   Or sullen brows that frown.

" Most lovely is the home of love,
   Where peace and pleasure dwell,
Fit emblems of the realms above,
   Where no fierce tumults swell."

THE GOLDEN RULE.

To do to all men as I would
   That they should do to me,
Will make me kind, and just, and good,
   And so I'll try to be.

RICH AND POOR.

OUR country house at Christmas time,
   It was a pleasant sight,
The holly hung in every room,
   The fires were blazing bright;
As the snow-clad hills around
   Came down the winter night.

My little brother George and I,
  Stood watching at the door,
To see our uncle's carriage come,
  And greet our cousins four;
When a poor hungry boy came near
  That only tatters wore.

He told how, once, his father toiled,
  But now was with the dead,
That there was sickness in his home,
  And bitter want of bread.
We gave him all our hoarded pence
  For the sad words he said.

But when our cousins came at last,
  And there was mirth to see,
The gilded gifts, and pretty toys,
  Hung on our Christmas tree;
I told my mother of the boy,
  And thus she said to me: —

" So much the more we owe to God,
  For all that he hath given,
A ready mind to help the hands
  That sore with want have striven,
Since they that are the poor on earth
  May be the rich in heaven."

PEASANT'S EVENING SONG.

COME to the sunset tree!
    The day is past and gone;
The woodman's axe lies free,
    And the reaper's work is done.

The twilight star to heaven
    And the summer dew to flowers,
And rest to us is given ·
    By the cool soft evening hours.

Sweet is the hour of rest;
　Pleasant the wind's low sigh;
And the gleaming of the west,
　And the turf whereon we lie.

When the burden and the heat
　Of labor's task are o'er,
And kindly voices greet
　The tired one at his door.

Come to the sunset tree!
　The day is past and gone;
The woodman's axe lies free,
　And the reaper's work is done.

Yes; tuneful is the sound
　That dwells in whispering boughs;
Welcome the freshness round,
　And the gale that fans our brows.

But rest more sweet and still
　Than ever nightfall gave,
Our yearning hearts shall fill
　In the world beyond the grave.

There shall no tempest blow,
　Nor scorching noontide heat;

There shall be no more snow
To weary, wandering feet.

So we lift our trusting eyes
From the hills our fathers trod,
To the quiet of the skies,
To the Sabbath of our God.

Come to the sunset tree!
The day is past and gone;
The woodman's axe lies free,
And the reaper's work is done.

Mrs. Hemans.

THE CLOCKING HEN.

" WILL you take a walk with me,
My little wife, to-day?
There's barley in the barley field,
And hayseed in the hay."

" Thank you," said the clocking hen,
" I've something else to do ·
I'm busy sitting on my eggs,
I cannot walk with you."

"Clock, clock, clock, clock,"
  Said the clocking hen;
"My little chicks will soon be hatched,
  "I 'll think about it then."

The clocking-hen sat on her nest,
  She made it in the hay;
And warm and snug beneath her breast,
  A dozen white eggs lay.

Crack, crack, went all the eggs,
  Out dropt the chickens small;
"Clock," said the clocking hen,
  "Now I have you all."

"Come along, my little chicks,
  I 'll take a walk with you;
"Hallo," said the barn-door cock.
  "Cock-a-doodle-doo."

———◆———

GOING TO BED.

Now I lay me down to sleep,
I pray the Lord my soul to keep;
If I should die before I wake,
I pray the Lord my soul to take.

HONESTY.

WITH honest heart go on your way,
   Down to your burial sod,
And never for a moment stray
   Beyond the path of God.

Then like a happy pilgrim here,
   O'er pleasant meadow going,
You 'll reach the bank without a fear,
   Where death's chill stream is flowing.

And every thing along your way
   In colors bright shall shine ;
The water from the jug of clay
   Shall taste like costly wine !

Then cherish faith and honesty
   Down to your burial clod,
And never for a moment stray
   Beyond the path of God.

Your sons and grandsons to your tomb
   Shall come, their tears to shed ;
And from their tears sweet flowers shall
     bloom,
   Above your sleeping head !

From the German.

THE CHILD AND THE LAMB.

MY pretty lamb, with snowy fleece,
    With low and tender bleat,
And feet that o'er the daisies fly
    So soundless and so fleet.
To meet me when I come in sight,
    Through sunshine or through showers;
How merry you and I have been
    Among the meadow flowers.

I never found you cross or tired,
    The whole long summer day ;
I never knew you leave my side,
    Nor yet refuse to play.
There 's none of all my schoolfellows
    That love me now like you ;
And I had many a pet before,
    But none that seemed so true.

They brought me in a robin once
    That had a broken wing ;
I nursed him all the winter, but
    He flew away in spring.
The next, it was a lovely squirrel,
    So full of tricks and fun,
But he left me in the wood one day,
    At the setting of the sun.

You will not leave me too, my lamb;
    But sometimes in my sleep
I grieve to dream that you have grown
    An old and quiet sheep;
That only minds the grass all day,
    And never lifts its eyes,
Like all your friends in yonder field,
    So woolly and so wise.

Thus talked poor Lucy, to her lamb,
    With arms about it twined,
Till her good father passed and spoke
    To her in words as kind:

" So must my little rosy girl,
  That now so blithely plays,
From childhood grow to woman's cares,
  To woman's works and ways.

" A world of hopes and fears, beyond
  Her early playmate's lot,
Awaits my Lucy, when her sports
  And pets are all forgot.
Yet may she still its innocence,
  Her fair example hold,
And live a meek and guileless lamb
  In our good Shepherd's fold."

THE ROOKS.

THE Rooks are building on the trees,
  They build there every spring;
" Caw, caw," is all they say,
  For none of them can sing.

They 're up before the break of day,
  And up till late at night ;
For they must labor busily
  As long as it is light.

And many a crooked stick they bring,
  And many a slender twig,

And many a tuft of moss, until
  Their nests are round and big.

"Caw, caw."   Oh, what a noise
  They make in rainy weather!
Good children always speak by turns,
  But Rooks all talk together.

How many nests are on the trees,
  And up at what a height!
There are a thousand Rooks, and yet
  I never saw them fight;

For they are friendly birds, and each
  Is to his neighbors known:
. They never touch each other's things,
  But let them all alone.

I wonder if we ever heard
  Of little girls and boys
Who quarrelled more than Rooks, and made
  A more unpleasant noise?

I wonder if we ever heard
  Of children who would touch
The things they ought to let alone —
  I wonder very much?

HUSH, MY BABE.

Hush, my babe, lie still and slumber;
  Holy angels guard thy bed;
Heavenly blessings without number,
  Gently falling on thy head.

Sleep, my babe, thy food and raiment,
  House and home, thy friends provide;
All without thy care or payment,
  All thy wants are well supplied.

See the lovely babe a dressing;
  Lovely infant, how he smiled:
When he wept, the mother's blessing
  Soothed and hushed the holy Child.

Lo, he slumbers in the manger,
  Where the horned oxen fed!
Peace, my darling, here's no danger,
  There's no oxen near thy bed.

'T was to save thee, child, from dying,
  Save my dear from burning flame,
Bitter groans and endless crying,
  That thy blest Redeemer came.

May'st thou live to know and fear him,
 Trust and love him all thy days;
Then go dwell forever near him,
 See his face and sing his praise.

I could give thee thousand kisses,
 Hoping what I most desire;
Not a mother's fondest wishes
 Can to greater joys aspire.

Dr. Watts.

THE FIRST WALK.

A WONDROUS venture it must be,
My trembling little one, for thee
 To trust thy feeble feet
Upon this hard old earth of ours;
And thou hast summoned all thy powers
 The mighty task to meet.

There's caution in that look of thine
And in the hand that clings to mine,
 With clasp so keen and small;
Yet thou wilt learn to jump and run
Through the green meadows in the sun,
 And never fear a fall.

These are thy faint first steps in life,
And though they seem with danger rife,
 The peril is not there;
But in thine after goings, child! —
For oh this world is wide and wild,
 And much more false than fair!

I cannot tell what stranger shore
These timid feet may journey o'er —
 What desert bleak and broad;
But I can truly hope and pray
That thou may'st walk in wisdom's way,
 And humbly with thy God.

———◆———

SUMMER.

THE sky is bright above,
 The lake is bright below;
The boatmen sail on merrily,
 All singing as they go.

The corn is ripening in the field,
 The fruit upon the bough,
The spring time gay has passed away,
 And it is summer now.

GATHERING WILD FLOWERS.

THEY were blithe times with us when the sum-
     mer had come,
With the nightingale's song, and the honey-
     bee's hum,
With lilies, and roses, and long sunny hours,
And holiday goings to gather wild flowers.

We went all together, one bright afternoon,
When warm on the woods lay the sunlight of
     June,
And up in the sky was a blueness, as clear
As if not a cloud had been there all the year.

Old grandmother went with her staff in her
  hand,
She said, " To see summer once more in the
  land ; "
While good uncle William walked cheerfully
  by,
And, we had such baskets, my sister and I

'T was sweet in the meadows, 't was sweet in
  the woods,
And great was our gathering of blossoms and
  buds,
By the banks of bright streams, by the roots
  of old trees,
Where nestled the wild birds, and feasted the
  bees.

Then home with light hearts and full baskets
  we sped,
When sunset was tinging the old church with
  red,
But paused at our gate to look back on the
  view,
How rich in the gold of the evening it grew.

And grandmother said, as she gazed on the
  sky,
With thoughts of her seventy long summers
  gone by,

" What glory must gladden that good land of
    ours,
When this earth is so fair in the time of wild
    flowers!"

———◆———

TWINKLE, TWINKLE, LITTLE STAR.

TWINKLE, twinkle, little star;
How I wonder what you are!
Up above the world so high,
Like a diamond in the sky.

When the glorious sun is set,
When the grass with dew is wet,
Then you show your little light,
Twinkle, twinkle, all the night.

In the dark blue sky you keep,
And often through my curtains peep;
For you never shut your eye
Till the sun is in the sky.

As your bright and tiny spark
Lights the traveller in the dark,
Though I know not what you are,
Twinkle, twinkle, little star.

THE CUCKOO.

AND so you have come back again,
 And it was you I heard
Proclaiming it to all the world —
 You most conceited bird.

You talked of nothing but yourself
 When you were here before,
Until your voice became so hoarse
 That you could talk no more.

And now you fly from bush to bush,
 And say " Cuckoo, cuckoo."
Have you no friends to care about?
No useful work to do?

I hear you 're such a lazy bird,
 You cannot build a nest;
Perhaps you could, if you would try —
 We ought to do our best.

The little bird that told me this,
 Suspected something worse, —
That you neglect your little ones,
 And put them out to nurse.

3

Oh, Cuckoo! if this story 's true,
 I think you 're much to blame.
Then talk no more about yourself
 So. Hide yourself, for shame.

———◆———

A BETTER SON.

An old man to our hearth had come,
 One evening in the time of snow,
He told us of his childhood's home,
 And of his parents long ago:
How much for him they worked and
 prayed —
 How long their toils and prayers were
 done;   .
And then the old man sighing, said,
 " If I had been a better son."

We never knew what early sin
 Called forth that aged traveller's sigh,
But often have I thought since then,
 My parents must grow old and die;
And mine may be a grief as keen
 For harsh words said, or follies done;
Therefore, my daily prayer has been
 That I might be a better son.

DING! DONG! BELL!

Ding! Dong! Bell!
  Why do you ring so clear?
In the early morning
  Sleep to me is dear.

'T is time you were up, little boy,
  Early rise if you wish to be well;
No sluggard can list to my song
  ·Of Ding! Dong! Bell!

Ding! Dong! Bell!
  Why do you ring at noon?
Making me stop my play
  To list to your cheerful tune.

For dinner 't is time, little boy,
  The laborers hurry pellmell;
Welcome to them is the sound
  Of Ding! Dong! Bell!

Ding! Dong! Bell!
  Again your solemn peal
In the early evening
  On my ear does steal.

Time you were in your bed, little boy,
    The end of day 1 knell;
Welcome to all is the evening sound
    Of Ding! Dong! Bell!

———◆———

THE YOUNG AND OLD.

GRANDFATHER dear, where are they gone,
    Those boys that were all at school with
        you,
Wrestling Richard, jumping John,
    Climbing Harry, and hardy Hugh;
We have heard of their doings many a
        day,
Grandfather, tell us where are they?

" My boy, it is sixty years ago,
    And all my schoolmates are dead and
        gone,
But the lame old man at the lodge you
        know,
    'T was he who was once called jumping
        John,
And I, whom the east wind pierces through,
Was the boy for the winters, hardy Hugh."

AUTUMN.

PEACHES ripe and apples mellow,
　　Grapes both sweet and clear,
Fill the dishes on the sideboard,
　　Tell that autumn's here.

'T is merry in the cornfield,
　　When harvest wagons stand ;
When to and fro the reapers go,
　　The sickle in their hand.

Then give we thanks to God,
    At even and at morn,
Who sent the spring and summer sun
    To ripen Autumn's corn.

—◆—

THE SUN.

SOMEWHERE it is always light;
    For when 't is morning here,
In some far distant land 't is night,
    And the bright moon shines there.

When you 're undressed and going to bed,
    They are just rising there;
And morning on the hills doth spread,
    When it is evening here.

And other distant lands there be,
    Where it is always night;
For weeks and weeks they never see
    The sun, nor have they light.

For it is dark both night and day;
    But what 's as wond'rous quite,
The darkness it doth pass away,
    And then for weeks 't is light.

Yes, while you sleep the sun shines bright,
 The sky is blue and clear;
For weeks and weeks there is no night,
 But always daylight there.

THE BIRD'S NEST.

Who would rob the linnet's nest,
Or its tender young molest,
Heedless of their chirping cries?
Naughty boy, restore the prize!

Thoughtless child! did you but know,
All the love and all the woe
That the parent birds must feel,
You would ne'er such treasures steal.

Helpless things, too young to
Captives in a cage they'll die!
Where's their mother, food to bring,
And enfold them with her wing?

Wailing in some lonely brake,
Broken-hearted for their sake,
Like a mourning mother left,
Of her children dear bereft!

God above who cares for all,
He who sees the sparrow fall,
Made them free on joyful wing,
Through the air to soar and sing.

————◆————

RIDE AWAY, RIDE

RIDE away, ride away, ride!
Away to the market we go,
Placed snugly the basket beside,
    With chickens set all in a row.

The sheep on the field that we see,
    May stare at our carriage so fine,
But there is not a lamb on the lea
    With a heart so delighted as thine.

Though lofty the gentle folks ride,
    With horses that canter and neigh,
Far safer and smoother we glide,
    And gather sweet flowers on the way.

The higher they caper and bound,
    The farther they sink when they fall,
But riding so near to the ground,
    The wheel-barrow's safest of all.

Ride away, ride away, ride!
We'll pull off the sweet-blooming thorn,
And daisies that deck the way side,
For garlands when home we return.

——◆——

AGAINST QUARRELLING AND FIGHTING.

LET dogs delight to bark and bite,
For God hath made them so;
Let bears and lions growl and fight,
For 't is their nature too.

But, children, you should never let
Such angry passions rise;
Your little hands were never made
To tear each other's eyes.

Let love through all your actions run,
And all your words be mild;
Live like the blessed Virgin's Son,
That sweet and lovely child.

His soul was gentle as a lamb;
And, as his stature grew,
He grew in favor both with man
And God his Father too.

Now, Lord of all, he reigns above,
    And from his heavenly throne,
He sees what children dwell in love,
    And marks them for his own.

THE COW.

THANK you, pretty cow, that made
Pleasant milk to soak my bread,
Every day and every night,
Warm, and fresh, and sweet, and white.

Do not chew the hemlock rank,
Growing on the weedy bank ;
But the yellow cowslips eat,
They will make it very sweet.

Where the purple violet grows,
Where the bubbling water flows,
Where the grass is fresh and fine,
Pretty cow, go there and dine.

LEARNING TO GO ALONE.

COME, my darling, come away,
Take a pretty walk to-day.

Run along, and never fear,
I 'll take care of baby dear.

Up and down with little feet,
That 's the way to *walk*, my sweet ;
Now it is so very near,
Soon she 'll get to mother dear.

There, she comes along at last ;
Here 's my finger, hold it fast :
Now one pretty little kiss,
After such a walk as this.

———◆———

I USED TO THINK.

I USED to think there would be fun
When all my going to school was done,
    And all my lessons o'er ;
When my good master— I thought him then
The worst and wildest of mortal men —
    Should hear my tasks no more.

Well, now, the school time is all past,
I 'm out of my master's thrall at last,
    And sent to business here.
Yet the days of grumbling are not gone,
Fortunes may change, but they last on,
    Still fresh from year to year.

GROWLER.

Go, naughty Growler, get away,
You shall not have a bit;

Now when I speak how dare you stay?
I can't spare any, sir, I say,
  And so you need not sit.

Poor Growler! do not make him go,
  But recollect, before,
That he has never served you so,
For you have given him many a blow
  That patiently he bore.

Poor Growler! if he could but speak,
  He'd tell (as well he might)
How he would bear with many a freak,
And wag his tail, and look so meek,
  And neither bark nor bite.

Upon his back he lets you ride,
  All round and round the yard;
And now, while sitting by your side,
To have a bit of bread denied,
  Is really very hard.

And all your little tricks he'll bear,
  And never seem to mind;
And yet you say you cannot spare
One bit of breakfast for his share,
  Although he is so kind!

LOOK UP, MY CHILD.

To yonder blue and boundless dome,
That bends o'er river, hill, and home,
Wherein the sun his circuit makes,
Where the mild moon by night awakes,
Where morning breaks, where evening falls,
From whence the mighty thunder calls —
Where rainbows rise, where clouds are piled
Above man's reach — Look up, my child.

That sky was all as brightly blue
When Adam gazed, and Eden grew,
Though centuries since then have rolled,
It has not altered, or grown old,
But speaks to every heart and eye
Of him who built its arch so high,
And spread it forth, o'er wave and wild,
To tell his praise — Look up, my child.

This earth, though it be fair to see,
With hill and valley, stream and tree,
Hath change without — hath graves within,
And many a trace of tears and sin.
Then lift thine eyes, and lift thy heart,
And seek beyond the skies thy part,
Where stands that city undefiled
Through life and death — Look up, my child.

GETTING UP.

Now, my baby, ope your eye,
For the sun is in the sky,
And he's peeping once again
Through the frosty window-pane;
Little baby, do not keep
Any longer fast asleep.

There now, sit in mother's lap,
That she may untie your cap;
For the little strings have got
Twisted into *such* a knot:
Ah! for shame, you've been at play
With the bobbin, as you lay.

There it comes, now let us see,
Where your petticoats can be:
Oh! they're in the window-seat,
Folded very smooth and neat:
When my baby older grows,
She shall double up her clothes.

Now one pretty little kiss,
For dressing you so nice as this;
And before you go down stairs,
Don't forget to say your prayers;
For 't is God who loves to keep
Little babies while they sleep.

THE LITTLE COWARD.

WHY, here 's a foolish little man!
Laugh at him, donkey, if you can;
And cat, and dog, and cow, and calf,
Come, every one of you, and laugh.

For only think, he runs away
If honest donkey does but bray!
And when the bull begins to bellow,
He 's like a crazy little fellow.

Poor Brindle cow can hardly pass
Along the hedge to nip the grass,
Or wag her tail to lash the flies,
But off he runs and loudly cries!

And when old Tray comes jumping too,
With bow, wow, wow, for how d 'ye do,
And means it all for civil play,
'T is sure to make him run away!

But all the while you 're thinking, may be,
"Ah! well, but this must be a baby."
Oh! cat, and dog, and cow, and calf,
I 'm not surprised to see you laugh,
He 's five years old and almost half.

THE CUT.

WELL, what's the matter? there's a face!
What! have you cut a vein?
And is it quite a shocking place?
Come, let us look again.

I see it bleeds, but never mind
That tiny little drop;
I don't believe you'll ever find
That crying makes it stop.

'T is sad indeed, to cry at pain,
For any but a baby;
If *that* should chance to cut a vein,
We should not wonder, may be.

But such a man as you should try
To bear a little sorrow:
So run about and wipe your eye,
'T will all be well to-morrow.

————◆————

THE WARNING.

UNDER a tree, and by a well,
There stands a cottage in yonder dell;
Within that cot live children three, .
Such children did you never see.

4

They quarrel at meals, they quarrel at play,
They quarrel, I'm told, both night and day;
For every one wants every thing,
And peace from the house has taken wing.

Their voices have got the quarreller's tone,
Their faces to quarreller's looks have grown;
Then lest you come to lead their life,
Brothers and sisters, cease from strife.

TEACH ME TO PRAY.

LORD, teach a little child to pray,
    And oh, accept my prayer!
Thou hearest all the words I say,
    For thou art everywhere.

A little sparrow cannot fall
    Unnoticed, Lord, by thee;
And though I am so young and small,
    Thou carest still for me.

Teach me to do whate'er is right,
    And when I sin, forgive;
And make it still my chief delight
    To love thee while I live.

THE CHILD'S QUESTIONS.

WHO made the pretty fields, mamma,
  With flowers red and blue ?
Who made the pretty stars, mamma ?
  And who made me and you ?

'T was God, my child, who made the world,
  And all things bright and fair ;
His goodness keeps us all from harm,
  His hand is everywhere.

And did he make the trees, mamma;
The rivers, and the sea;
And the bright sun that from the sky
Shines down so cheerfully?

And can God see us all, mamma,
And hear each word we say?
And does he see me when I sleep,
And when I sing and play?

He sees us all, my little one,
From his bright throne above;
And stretches o'er us, day by day,
The shelter of his love.

High on his heavenly throne he hears
Each little prayer you say;
Then learn to love him, little child,
And seek him day by day.

THE LITTLE BABY.

WHAT is this pretty little thing,
That nurse so carefully doth bring,
And round its head her apron fling?
             A baby!

Oh! dear, how very soft its cheek:
Why, Nurse, I cannot make it speak,
And it can't walk, it is so weak,
                    Poor baby.

Here, take a bit, you little dear,
I've got nice cake and sweetmeats here:
'T is very nice, you need not fear,
                    You baby.

Oh! I'm afraid that it will die ;
Why can't it eat as well as I,
And jump and talk ?   Do let it try,
                    Poor baby.

Why, you were once a baby too,
And could not jump as now you do,
But good mamma took care of you,
                    Like baby.

And then she taught your pretty feet
To pat along the carpet neat,
And call papa to come and meet
                    His baby.

Oh! dear mamma to take such care,
And no kind pains and trouble spare,
To feed and nurse you when you were
                    A baby.

THE FISHING BOAT.

I KNOW a little fishing boat
    That puts out every night,
To take the fishes in the sea,
    When the moon is shining bright.

And when the clouds are in the sky,
    And winds are whistling shrill,
This little fishing boat puts out
    From the haven by the hill.

What makes the fisherman go out
    In wind and storm, as well
As when the weather's calm and fair?
    I fancy I can tell.

I 've seen three little children,
    That stood upon the shore,
To watch the fishing boat come in ; —
    They watched an hour and more.

And when, at last, they saw it come,
    The youngest of them said,
" Here 's daddy coming home, at last ;
    And now we shall have bread."

· And that is why the fishing boat
  Went every night to sea ; —
  The father had to earn the bread
  To feed those children three.

———◆———

THE PET GOAT.

A FLOWERY chaplet wreathes her head,
  While innocence and love,
That in her breast their home have made,
  Have brighter garlands wove.

The Goat and Dog are all her care
  When shine the sunny hours,
And with her loved companions there,
  She plays among the flowers.

The Goat's rough head and branching horns
  She decks with streamers gay,
And many a pendant flower adorns
  His flowing beard of gray.

But better far he loves the crumbs
  Her little hand bestows,
And runs to meet her when she comes,
  And sorrows when she goes.

The Dog springs up and barks for joy
    With pretty Jane to rove,
And views the Goat with jealous eye,
    A rival for her love.

———◆———

THE SLUGGARD.

'T is the voice of the sluggard, — I heard him
    complain,
" You have waked me too soon ; I must slum-
    ber again : "
As the door on its hinges, so he on his bed
Turns his sides and his shoulders, and his
    heavy head.

" A little more sleep, and a little more slum-
    ber ; "
Thus he wastes half his days, and his hours
    without number ;
And when he gets up, he sits folding his
    hands,
Or walks about saunt'ring, or trifling he
    stands.

I passed by his garden, and saw the wild briar,
The thorn and the thistle, grow broader and
    higher ;

The clothes that hang on him are turning to
    rags,
And his money still wastes, 'till he starves or
    he begs.

I made him a visit, still hoping to find
That he took better care for improving his
    mind ;
He told me his dreams, talked of eating and
    drinking ;
But he scarce reads his Bible, and never loves
    thinking.

THE BABY'S DANCE.

DANCE, little baby, dance up high :
Never mind, baby, mother is nigh ;
Crow and caper, caper and crow,
There, little baby, there you go ;
Up to the ceiling, down to the ground,
Backwards and forwards, round and round,
Then dance, little baby, and mother shall sing,
While the gay merry coral goes ding, ding
    a-ding, ding.

LITTLE THINGS.

LITTLE drops of water,
Little grains of sand,
Make the mighty ocean,
And the pleasant land.

Thus the little minutes,
Humble though they be,
Make the mighty ages
Of eternity.

Thus our little errors
Lead the soul away,
From the path of virtue
Off in sin to stray.

Little deeds of kindness,
Little words of love,
Make our earth an Eden,
Like the heaven above.

THE NAUGHTY SISTER.

Go, go, my naughty girl, and kiss
  Your little sister dear;
I must not have such scenes as this,
  And noisy quarrels here.

What! little children scratch and fight,
  That ought to be so mild!
Oh! Mary, it 's a shocking sight
  To see an angry child.

I can't imagine, for my part,
  The reason of your folly;
She did not do you any harm,
  By playing with your dolly.

See, see, the little tears that run
  Fast from her watery eye;
Come, my sweet innocent, be done,
  'Twill do no good to cry.

Go, Mary, wipe her tears away,
  And make it up with kisses;
And never turn a pretty play
  To such a pet as this is.

THE AIR-BUBBLE.

Blow the bubble, happy boy,
And thy fleeting sport enjoy;
Globe of azure, gold and green,
Brighter bubble ne'er was seen!

Silly thing of froth and air,
Off it goes! we know not where:
While another follows fast,
Bright and transient as the last.

Such are oft the dreams of youth,
Airy phantoms, void of truth;
Such the schemes of riper age,
When the world's delusions rage.

Life's a bubble at the best, —
Clouds where air-built castles rest,
Schemes by vain ambition nurst,
Like the airy bubble burst.

Blow the bubble, happy child,
You at least are not beguiled:
Pretty pastime, — better far
Than the world's great bubbles are.

THE GREAT BROWN OWL.

THE brown Owl sits in the ivy bush,
   And she looketh wondrous wise,
With a horny beak beneath her cowl,
   And a pair of large round eyes.

She sat all day on the self-same spray,
   From sunrise till sunset;
And the dim, grey light it was all too bright
   For the owl to see in yet.

" Jenny-Owlet, Jenny-Owlet," said a merry
     little bird,
  " They say you're wondrous wise;
But I don't think you see, though you're
     looking at ME
With your large, round, shining eyes."

But night came soon, and the pale white moon
   Rolled high up in the skies;
And the great brown Owl flew away in her
     cowl,
   With her large, round, shining eyes.

THE OLD CLOCK.

Listen to the kitchen clock!
 To itself it ever talks,
 From its place it never walks;
" Tick-tock — tick-tock."
  Tell me what it says.

" I 'm a very patient clock,
 Never moved by hope or fear,
 Though I 've stood for many a year;
Tick-tock — tick-tock."
  That is what it says.

" I 'm a very truthful clock:
 People say, about the place,
 Truth is written on my face;
Tick-tock — tick-tock."
  That is what it says.

" I 'm a very active Clock,
 For I go while you 're asleep,
 Though you never take a peep;
Tick-tock — tick-tock."
  That is what it says.

" I 'm a most obliging Clock :
　If you wish to hear me strike,
　You may do it when you like ;
Tick-tock — tick-tock."
　　That is what it says.

What a talkative old Clock !
　Let us see what it will do
　When the pointer reaches two ;
' Ding-ding " — " tick-tock."
　　That is what it says.

POLITENESS.

Good boys and girls will never say,
　" *I will*," and " *Give me* these ;"
Oh, no ; that never is the way,
　But, " Mother, if you please."

And " *If you please*," to sister Ann,
　Good boys to say are ready ;
And " *Yes sir*," to a gentleman,
　And " *Yes ma'am*," to a lady.

GERTRUDE AND HER ALPHABET.

You have not heard the story yet
Of Gertrude and her Alphabet.
She learnt her letters from a board ;
As yet, she could not read a word,
But stood beside her mother's knee,
Who pointed out great **A B C**.

" I cannot see," said little Gerty ;
" Mamma, I think the board is dirty !"
" No, not at all," her mother said ;
" The letters are jet black and red,
On snow-white paper ; — nay, be wise,
You cannot see with tearful eyes."

But still the tear-drops, large and round, ,
Go trickling slowly to the ground,

And all the letters, great and small,
Seem to move with them as they fall.
The crystal drops on her eyelashes
Quiver with black and scarlet dashes.

"Strange," thought the child, "I always
      thought
That was round O, when I was taught,
Yet now it turns into a loop,
And now — into my own new hoop!
That hoop-stick once was little I;
I'm sure it was, I knew it well."

The child is looking at a tear,
Which, like a mirror bright and clear,
Reflects the letters as they pass,
As on the Fairy's magic glass;
And all the little dingy letters
Bow to the red ones, as their betters.

Q started, and turned up its tail;
H turned into a hurdle-rail;
And i, with its droll little head,
Lay down on B, which stands for bed;
While p, which always puzzled you,
Turned round and mimicked little q.

5

a, with its puffed out paunch,
    looked odd,
And turned into a Chinese
    god ;
u was a washing tub ; but
    then,
Turned upside down, they
    called it **n**.
And both the great and little **K**'s
Kicked out their feet and laughed at **T**'s.

The **W**'s turned over soon,
And then they looked like **M** for moon ;
And both the crooked **S**'s, they
Ran up a step-ladder, great **A** ;
While **X** and **Z** and **D** and **T**
Looked like themselves, and so did **V**.

Small **h** looked like the high backed chairs ;
Y like a wine-glass — Gerty stares
To see **a** imitating **b**,
Its cousin-german — as for **g**,
A pair of spectacles it grows,
And mounts on little Gerty's nose !

" Well, can you see them now, my child ? "
Her mother asked, in accents mild.

The tear-drops fall from Gertrude's eyes,
The magic mirror vanishes,
And little Gertrude laughs, " Ha, ha!
I know my letters, now, Mamma."

———◆———

SLEEPY HARRY.

" I DO not like to go to bed,"
Sleepy little Harry said,
" Go, naughty Betty, go away,
I will not come at all, I say ! "

Oh, what a little silly fellow !
I should be quite ashamed to tell her;
Then, Betty, you must come and carry
This very foolish little Harry.

The little birds are better taught,
They go to roosting when they ought;
And all the ducks, and fowls, you know,
They went to bed an hour ago.

The little beggar in the street,
Who wanders with his *naked* feet,
And has not where to lay his head,
Oh, he'd be *glad* to go to bed.

THE EVENING PRAYER.

In the solemn shade of the twilight sky,
Which tells of another day gone by,
In the hush of thy home, so calm and free,
Thou art kneeling, child! at thy mother's knee.

And they that kneel in the proudest fane,
Of sculptured pillar, and pictured pane,
Of breathing censer, and jewelled shrine,
Have found no altar more blest than thine.

For there thou hast learned to praise His
        might,
Who guides the march of the day and night:
And there thou hast learned to seek his grace,
Who makes with the meek his dwelling-place.

Say, will that lesson long abide
When thou art far from thy mother's side,
When the hair is gray — or the grave is green
Of her, that thine earliest love has been.

When the snares of life are around thee set,
And the cares have come which thou knowest
        not yet;

When business calls thee at early day,
And memories deepen the evening's gray.

Whate'er the course of thine after track,
Whate'er the change, will thy heart come back,
In spite of sin, and in spite of snare,
To thy mother's knee and thine evening
    prayer!

—◆—

GOING TO BED.

Down upon my pillow warm,
  I do lay my little head,
And the rain, and wind, and storm,
  Cannot come too nigh my bed.

Dear mamma, I thank you oft
  For this comfortable bed,
And this pretty pillow soft,
  Where I rest my little head.

I shall sleep till morning light,
  On a bed so nice as this;
So, my dear mamma, good-night,
  Give your little girl a kiss.

LITTLE RAIN-DROPS.

WHERE do you come from,
   You little drops of rain,
Pitter patter, pitter patter,
   Down the window pane ?

They won't let me walk,
   And they won't let me play,
And they won't let me go
   Out of doors at all to-day.

They put away my playthings .
   Because I broke them all,
And then they locked up all my bricks,
   And took away my ball.

Tell me, little rain-drops,
   Is that the way you play,
Pitter patter, pitter patter,
   All the rainy day?

They say I'm very naughty,
   But I've nothing else to do,
But sit here at the window;
   I should like to play with you.

The little rain drops cannot speak,
   But "pitter, pitter pat"
Means, we can play on *this* side,
   Why can't you play on that?

---◆---

THE CHERRY-TREE.

FREDDIE saw some fine ripe cherries
   Hanging on a cherry-tree;
And he said, "You pretty cherries,
   Will you not come down to me?"

"Thank you kindly," said a cherry,
   "We would rather stay up here;
If we ventured down this morning,
   You would eat us up, I fear."

One, the finest of the cherries,
   Dangling from a slender twig;

" You are beautiful," said Freddie,
    " Red and ripe, and oh, how big ! "

" Catch me," said the cherry, " catch me,
    Little master, if you can ! "
" I would catch you soon," said Freddie,
    " If I were a grown up man."

Freddie jumped and tried to reach it,
    Standing high upon his toes ;
But the cherry bobbed about,
    And laughed and tickled Freddie's nose.

" Never mind," said little Freddie,
    " I shall have them when it's right,"
But a blackbird whistled boldly,
    " I shall eat them all to-night."

———◆———

THE VAIN LITTLE GIRL.

WHAT ! looking in the glass again !
Why is my silly child so vain ?
Do you think yourself as fair
As the gentle lilies are ?

Is your merry eye as blue
As the violet's, wet with dew ?
Yet it loves the best to hide
By the hedge's shady side.

When your cheek the brightest glows,
Is it redder than the rose?
But the rose's buds are seen
Almost hid with moss and green.

Little flowers, that open gay,
Peeping forth at break of day,
In the garden, hedge, or plain,
Do you think that *they* are vain?

———————

BABY AND MAMMA.

What a little thing am I!
  Hardly higher than the table;
I can eat, and play, and cry,
  But to work I am not able.

Nothing in the world I know,
  But mamma will try and show me;
Sweet mamma, I love her so,
  She's so very kind unto me.

And she sets me on her knee
  Very often for some kisses:
Oh! how good I'll try to be,
  For such a dear mamma as this is.

THE SOLDIER.

" OH, I wish I was a soldier,
So gallant and so bold,
To ride upon a noble horse,
All trimmed with shining gold.

" To lead my men to battle,
At the loud drum's stirring call,
And charge upon the enemy,
Nor fear the leaden ball.

" And when the battle's over,
How proudly I'd return ;
The ' triumphs of a conqueror,'
Upon my cheeks would burn."

" But ah ! my son, you have forgot,
Upon the bloody ground,
At the close of every battle,
A heap of slain are found.

" And wounded too, and dying
On the cold and bloody ground,
. Far away from home and kindred,
Not a friend to stanch a wound.

" No kind and gentle mother,
To bless her darling child,
Or whisper hope and comfort,
On that field so sad and wild.

" Never. wish to be a soldier,
'T is a life to be abhorred ;
But let thy aim be higher,
Be a soldier of the Lord."

THE LITTLE CHILD.

I 'M a very little child,
    Only just have learned to speak ;
So I should be very mild,
    Very tractable and meek.

If my dear mamma were gone,
    I should perish soon, and die,
When she left me all alone,
    Such a little thing as I !

Oh, what service can I do,
    To repay her for her care ?
For I cannot even sew,
    Nor make any thing I wear.

Oh, then, I will always try
    To be very good and mild ;
Never now be cross and cry,
    Like a fretful little child.

For sometimes I cry and fret,
    And my dear mamma I tease ;
Or I vex her, while I sit
    Playing pretty on her knees.

Oh, how can I serve her so,
    Such a good mamma as this!
Round her neck my arms I'll throw,
    And her gentle cheeks I'll kiss.

Then I'll tell her that I will
    Try not any more to fret her,
And as I grow older still,
    Try to show I love her better.

———◆———

THE SPARROW AT THE WINDOW.

COME, give him, child, a bread crumb;
    For all the hills are bare, —
No rustle in the cornfield,
    No music in the air.

The flowers all are withered,
    The leaves are lying dead,
And now the thriftless sparrow
    Comes begging for his bread.

The little merry squirrel
    Hath hoarded up his store, —
He's nuts enough to last him
    Till summer comes once more.

He knew the time was coming
    When he must needs be fed ;
But, idling through the summer,
    The sparrow now wants bread.

Child, feed him, — he is hungry ;
    But take for thee this truth, —
The spring of life is childhood,
    Its summer day is youth.

Lay up in spring and summer
    A store from learning's page,
For the autumn hour of manhood, —
    The winter time of age.

——◆——

THE YOUNG LINNETS.

DID you ever see the nest
    Of Chaffinch or of Linnet,
When the little downy birds
    Are lying snugly in it,

Gaping wide their yellow mouths
    For something nice to eat?
Caterpillar, worm, and grub,
    They reckon dainty meat.

When the mother bird returns,
　And finds them still and good,
She will give them each by turns
　A proper share of food.

She has hopped from spray to spray,
　And peeped with knowing eye
Into all the folded leaves
　Where caterpillars lie.

She has searched among the grass,
　And flown from tree to tree,
Catching gnats and flies, to feed
　Her little family.

I have seen the Linnets chirp,
　And shake their downy wings ·
They are pleased to see her come,
　And pleased with what she brings.

But I never saw them look
　Impatient for their food.
Somebody, at dinner time,
　Is seldom quite so good.

ROBIN'S WELCOME.

THE summer leaves have perished,
    The harvest corn is gone,
Thy head can find no shelter
    When the heavy storm comes on.

But in our dwelling waits thee
    A welcome kind and free,
And while there 's bread among us
    We have a crumb for thee.

Thou hast sung beside our door, Robin,
    When the spring was drawing near;
Thou hast cheered our fading garden
    In the leaf-fall of the year.

From cottage, roof, or ruin,
   From tree-top bare and brown ;
Like a voice sent back from summer
   Thy silvery notes came down.

Through many a land and age, Robin,
   The children know thee thus :
Thou wert welcome to our fathers,
   Thou art welcome now to us.

And men of toil and travel
   In far off lands that roam,
Still greet thee as the household friend,
   The kindly bird of home.

Come in from the fierce wind, Robin,
   And from the drifting snow ;
Thou shalt have rest and refuge,
   Thou shalt be free to go.

And when the evenings brighten,
   And winter slacks his reign ;
Before the violet blossoms
   Thou shalt sing to us again.

6

PUSSY-CAT.

PUSSY-CAT lives in the servant's hall,
    She can set up her back, and purr;
The little mice live in a crack in the wall,
    But they hardly dare venture to stir;

For whenever they think of taking the air,
    Or filling their little maws,
The Pussy-Cat says, " Come out, if you dare;
    I will catch you all with my claws."

Scrabble, scrabble, scrabble, went all the little
        mice,
    For they smelt the Cheshire cheese;
The Pussy-Cat says, " It smells very nice,
    Now, DO come out, if you please."

" Squeak," said the little mouse; "squeak,
        squeak, squeak,"
    Said all the young ones too;
" We never creep out when cats are about,
    Because we're afraid of YOU."

So the cunning old Cat lay down on a mat
    By the fire in the servants' hall:

"If the little mice peep, they'll think I'm
  asleep;"
So she rolled herself up like a ball.

"Squeak," said the little mouse, "we'll
  creep out
And eat some Cheshire cheese,
That silly old Cat is asleep on the mat,
And we may sup at our ease."

Nibble, nibble, nibble went all the little mice,
  And they licked their little paws;
Then the cunning old Cat sprang up from the
  mat,
And caught them all with her claws.

——◆——

THE TURTLE-DOVE'S NEST.

VERY high in the pine-tree,
  The little Turtle-dove
Made a pretty little nursery,
  To please her little love.

She was gentle, she was soft,
  And her large dark eye
Often turned to her mate,
  Who was sitting close by.

"Coo," said the Turtle-dove.
"Coo," said she.
"Oh, I love thee," said the Turtle-dove.
"And I love THEE."

In the long shady branches
　　Of the dark pine-tree,
How happy were the doves
　　In their little nursery!

The young turtle-doves
　　Never quarrelled in the nest;
For they dearly loved each other,
　　Though they loved their mother best.

"Coo," said the little doves.
"Coo," said she.
And they played together kindly
　　In the dark pine-tree.

Is this nursery of yours,
　　Little sister, little brother,
Like the Turtle-dove's nest—
　　Do you love one another?

Are you kind, are you gentle,
　　As children ought to be?
Then the happiest of nests
　　Is your own nursery.

MY SISTER.

Is there a tie of human birth
Has more of heaven and less of earth
Than home-born love, the first and best
That warms a gentle sister's breast,
Who makes the little ones her care,
And loves their pretty sports to share?

Like dew upon the tender flower,
Her gentle words of truth and power,
With wonder, love, and joy combined,
Fall on her little brother's mind;
And thoughts that spring from home-born
    love
Point to the Better Land above.

THE WATER-MILL.

"ANY grist for the Mill?"
   How merrily it goes!
Flap, flap, flap, flap,
   While the water flows.
Round-about and round-about,
   The heavy mill-stones grind,
And the dust flies all about the mill,
   And makes the Miller blind.

"Any grist for the Mill?"
   The jolly farmer packs
His wagon with a heavy load
   Of very heavy sacks.
Noisily, oh noisily,
   The mill-stones turn about;
You cannot make the Miller hear
   Unless you scream and shout.

"Any grist for the Mill?"
   The bakers come and go;
They bring their empty sacks to fill,
   And leave them down below.
The dusty Miller and his men
   Fill all the sacks they bring,
And while they go about their work,
   Right merrily they sing.

" Any grist for the Mill ? "
How quickly it goes round !
Splash, splash, splash, splash,
   With a whirring sound.
Farmers, bring your corn to-day ;
   And bakers, buy your flour ;
Dusty millers, work away, ˙
   While it is in your power.

" Any grist for the Mill ? "
   Alas ! it will not go ;
The river, too, is standing still,
   The ground is white with snow.
And when the frosty weather comes,
   And freezes up the streams,
The Miller only hears the Mill,
   And grinds the corn in dreams.

Living close beside the Mill,
   The Miller's girls and boys
Always play at make-believe,
   Because they have no toys.
" Any grist for our Mill ? "
   The elder brothers shout,
While all the little Petticoats
   Go whirling round about.

The Miller's little boys and girls
  Rejoice to see the snow.
" Good father, play with us to-day ;
  You cannot work, you know.
We will be the mill-stones,
  And you shall be the wheel ;
We'll pelt each other with the snow,
  And it shall be the meal."

Oh, heartily the Miller's wife
  Is laughing at the door ;
She never saw the mill worked
  So merrily before.
" Bravely done, my little lads,
  Rouse up the lazy wheel,
For money comes but slowly in
  When snow-flakes are the meal."

———◆——

CHRIST'S HUMILITY.

CHRIST is merciful and mild ;
He was once a little child ;
He whom heavenly hosts adore,
Lived on earth among the poor.

Then he laid his glory by,
When for us he came to die;
How I wonder when I see
His unbounded love for me.

Through his life on earth I see,
Lowliness and poverty;
Oh how mean was his abode,
Though he was the mighty God!

Children in his arms he pressed,
Kindly took them to his breast;
They, said he, shall share my bliss,
For of such my kingdom is.

———◆———

GOD KEEPS ME.

FROM His high throne above the sky,
The Lord can all things see;
I cannot see Him, but His eye
Looks kindly down on me.

He cared for me before I knew
That I had such a friend;
When my first feeble breath I drew,
He did my life defend.

He keeps me still by His great power,
   From danger night and day ;
I could not live a single hour
   If he were far away.

But He is always near and kind,
   And loves to hear my prayer ;
May I His tender mercy find,
   And trust His love and care.

———◆———

PRAISE FOR MERCIES SPIRITUAL AND TEMPORAL.

Whene'er I take my walks abroad,
   How many poor I see !
What shall I render to my God,
   For all his gifts to me ?

Not more than others I deserve,
   Yet God hath given more ;
For I have food, while others starve,
   Or beg from door to door.

How many children in the street,
   Half naked I behold !
While I am clothed from head to feet,
   And covered from the cold.

While some poor wretches scarce can tell
   Where they may lay their head;
I have a home wherein to dwell,
   And rest upon my bed.

While others early learn to swear,
   And curse, and lie, and steal;
Lord, I am taught thy name to fear,
   And do thy holy will.

Are these thy favors day by day,
   To me above the rest?
Then let me love thee more than they,
   And strive to serve thee best.

GOD ORDERS ALL THINGS.

I THANK the Lord for all his grace
    To me so freely shown ;
At all times, and in every place,
    His goodness let me own.

It was not chance that placed me here,
    Where I am trained and taught
My Maker's name to know and fear,
    And love him as I ought.

The Lord in wisdom ordered where
    And when my birth should be,
And ever since with tender care
    He has watched over me.

He gives me all things ; day by day
    Fresh mercies does he send ;
And if I sin them not away,
    He will be still my friend.

———◆———

THE ROBIN REDBREASTS.

Two Robin Redbreasts built their nests
    Within a hollow tree ;

The hen sat quietly at home,
The cock sang merrily;
And all the little young ones said,
" Wee, wee, wee, wee, wee, wee."

One day (the sun was warm and bright,
And shining in the sky),
Cock-robin said, " My little dears,
'T is time you learn to fly ; "
And all the little young ones said,
" I 'll try, I 'll try, I 'll try."

I know a child, and who she is
I 'll tell you by and by,
When Mamma says, " Do this," or " that,"
She says, " What for ? " and " Why ? "
She 'd be a better child by far
If she would say, " I 'll try."

———◆———

THE BIBLE STORY.

ONCE among a band of brothers
There was one, his father's joy,
Loved so fondly that the others
Looked with envy on the boy,
For his kindness and his goodness
Treated him with scorn and rudeness.

In a desert place they threw him
   Down a pit, a living grave,
And when up again they drew him
   'T was to sell him for a slave,
To a life of want and danger
In the country of the stranger.

See him there by all forsaken,
   Fettered in a dungeon lie,
Yet he keeps his trust unshaken,
   And his Father hears his cry,
Lifts him out of tribulation
To a great and princely station.

Years went by, and to that city
   In distress his brethren came,
Then, unknown, he showed them pity,
   Never spoke a word of blame,
But by words and deeds of kindness
Made them weep their guilt and blindness.

In your youth like him endeavor
   Thus to know and love the Lord,
Choose his service, seek his favor,
   Follow Christ, and hear his word —
Once this heavenly Friend possessing,
You will want no other blessing.

OUR GARDEN.

It was gay in the spring-time of the year,
  It was fair at autumn's close ;
We heard the earliest cuckoo there,
  And we saw the latest rose.

The heart-ease and forget-me-not,
  They were natives of that ground ;
Our garden was the sunniest spot
  In all the country round.

There was many a quaint and bowery nook,
  Where we sat in summer's heat,
And listened to the silvery brook,
  That murmured at our feet.

There were herbs of old belief and fame,
    There were hives of busy bees,
And a swell of leafy sounds, that came
    When the wind was in the trees

We had little gardens every one,
    Myself and my brothers two,
And my sister, who is dead and gone;
    But the best of all it grew.

I cannot tell if the primrose time
    Comes now, as we knew it then;
But still in the April nights I dream
    We are there at work again.

The merry swing and the mossy well
    Were hard by my mother's bower,
Where the morning rose and the evening fell
    Through a screen of leaf and flower.

And pleasant was old Robin's pride
    In the seasons he had known,
And the long long years that by his side
    The silent flowers had grown.

He said the hawthorn hedge had put
    Forth near a hundred Mays,

And boughs from the holly he had cut
For fifty Christmas days;

That the cedar stood as large and tall
At the time when he was young,
And ever since in the ivy wall
Had his namesake built and sung.

The turf above old Robin's breast
Is lying green and cold;
The home and the garden we loved best
To a stranger's hand are sold.

He has planted hops where the roses grew,
He has hewn the cedar down;
And we look out all summer through
On the streets of this great town.

———•———

A COBWEB MADE TO ORDER.

A HUNGRY Spider made a web
Of thread so very fine,
Your tiny fingers scarce could feel
The little slender line.
Round-about, and round-about
And round-about it spun,
Straight across and back again
Until the web was done.

7

Oh, what a pretty shining web
  It was, when it was done!
The little flies all came to see
  It hanging in the sun.
     Round-about, and round-about,
      And round-about they danced,
    Across the web and back again
      They darted and they glanced.

The hungry Spider sat and watched
  The happy little flies;
It saw all round about its head,
  It had so many eyes.
     Round-about, and round-about,
      And round-about they go,
    Across the web and back again,
      Now high — now low.

"I am hungry, very hungry,"
  Said the Spider to a fly.
"If you were caught within the web,
  You very soon should die."
     But round-about, and round-about,
      And round-about once more,
    Across the web and back again
      They flitted as before.

For all the flies were much too wise
  To venture near the Spider;
They flapped their little wings and flew
  In circles rather wider.
      Round-about, and round-about,
        And round-about went they,
      Across the web and back again,
        And then they flew away.

THE LADY-BIRD.

LADY-BIRD, Lady-bird, warm is the day,
  And still in your cloak you come out;
Are your underneath wings, pray, so choice,
  That you wrap them so closely about?

The wings that you fly with, I know,
  Are not of a delicate hue;
For sometimes when you 're folding them up,
  There 's a small piece left out to the view.

I suppose 't is because they are thin,
  With care they are hidden away;
That their value consists in their use,
  So nature the cover made gay.

Then, Lady-bird, — still I may look,
  On your shining red cloak with delight,
Admiring its pretty black spots,
  To you useful, while pleasant to sight.

You're related, my brother has learnt,
  To the beetle-tribe, — some of which fly :
Beetles, many do brilliant coats wear,
  There are others, like yours, of red dye.

—◆—

GOOD-NIGHT.

LITTLE baby, lay your head
On your pretty cradle-bed ;
Shut your eye-peeps, now the day,
And the light has gone away ;
All the clothes are tucked in tight ;
Little baby dear, good-night.

Yes, my darling, well I know
How the bitter wind doth blow ;
And the winter's snow and rain
Patter on the window-pane,
But they cannot come in here
To my little baby dear :

For the window shutteth fast,
Till the stormy night is past ;
And the curtains warm are spread
Round about her cradle-bed :
So, till morning shineth bright,
Little baby dear, good-night.

MY BOAT ON THE LAKE.

I once made a boat at the midsummer time,
    When our lake was so glassy and still,
I was proud of her build, I was proud of her
    trim,
    And rejoiced in the might of my skill.
She was small, and her timbers were not over
    strong,
    But I thought they might weather a blast;
A pair of white sails bore her gaily along,
    And a red flag flew high from the mast.

I launched her in triumph! my young sisters
    stood
  In wonder the voyage to see ;
Poor Watch too was there, saying, plain as he
    could,
  There will none of you drown without me.
She went like the wind, and my glory was
    high,
  As a monarch's might be in his crown,
But just in the middle, I never knew why,
  The light vessel heeled and went down.

With her disappeared the delight of that day —
  The hope of my holidays all —   [play —
The labor of hours that were borrowed from
  The savings so prized and so small.   [spot
Poor Watch, at my bidding, plunged in at the
  Where last we had seen her afloat,
The dog came to shore again weary and wet,
  But he never could bring back the boat.

Since then I have steered a good ship on the
    sea,
  I 've weathered the winds of the world,
And seen the red cross from the mast flying
    free,
  When around it the cannon smoke curled.

I 've learned to take wisely life's sunshine or
    gale;
I trust a fair haven to make;
But many a brave hope, that went out in full
    sail,
Has gone down like my boat on the lake.

——◆——

THE PET LAMB.

ONCE on a time, a shepherd lived
    Within a cottage small;
The gray thatched roof was shaded by
    An elm-tree dark and tall;
While all around stretched far away
    A wild and lonesome moor,
Except a little daisied field
    Before the trellised door.

Now it was on a cold March day,
    When on the moorland wide,
The shepherd found a trembling lamb
    By its dead mother's side;
And so pitiful it bleated,
    As with the cold it shook,
He wrapped it up beneath his coat,
    And home the poor lamb took.

He placed it by the warm fire-side,
    And then his children fed
This little lamb, whose mother died,
    With milk and sweet brown bread,
Until it ran about the floor,
    Or at the door would stand;
And grew so tame it ate its food
    From out the children's hand.

It followed them where'er they went,
    Came ever at their call,
And dearly was this pretty lamb
    Beloved by them all.
And often on a market-day,
    When cotters crossed the moor,
They stopped to praise the snow-white
      lamb
    Beside the cottage door;
They patted it upon its head,
    And stroked it with the hand,
And vowed it was the prettiest lamb
    They'd seen in all the land.

Now this kind shepherd was as ill,
    As ill as he could be,
And kept his bed for many a week,
    And nothing earnéd he;

And when he had got well again,
  He to his wife did say,
" The doctor wants his money, and
  I have n't it to pay.

" What shall we do, what can we do ?
  The doctor 's made me well,
There 's only one thing can be done,
  We must the pet lamb sell ;
We 've nearly eaten all the bread,
  And how can we get more,
Unless you call the butcher in,
  When he rides by the door ? "

" Oh, do not sell my white pet lamb,"
  Then little Mary said,
" And every night I 'll go up stairs
  Without my tea to bed ;
For if the butcher buys my lamb,
  He 'll take away its life,
And make its pretty white throat bleed,
  With his sharp cruel knife ;

" And never in the morning light
  Again it will me meet,
Nor come again to lick my hand,
  Look up to me and bleat.

Oh, do not sell my sweet pet lamb;
　And if you'll let it live,
The best half of my bread and milk
　I will unto it give."
The doctor at that very time
　Entered the cottage door,
As, with her arms around her lamb,
　She sat upon the floor.

" Why do you weep, my pretty girl?"
　The doctor then did say.
" Because I love my little lamb,
　Which must be sold to-day ;
It lies beside my bed at night, —
　And, oh, it is so still,
It never made a bit of noise
　When father was so ill.

Oh, do not let them sell my lamb,
　And then I'll go to bed,
And never ask for aught to eat
　But a small piece of bread."
" I'll buy the lamb and give it you,"
　The kind good doctor said,
" And with the money that I pay,
　Your father can buy bread.

"As for the bill, that can remain
    Until another year."
He paid the money down, and said,
    "The lamb is yours, my dear.
You have a kind and gentle heart,
    And God, who made us all,
He loveth well those who are kind
    To creatures great and small;

"And while I live, my little girl,
    Your lamb shall not be sold,
But play with you upon the moor,
    And sleep within the fold."
And so the white pet lamb was saved,
    And played upon the moor,
And after little Mary ran
    About the cottage floor.

It fed upon the cowslips tall,
    And ate the grass so sweet,
And on the little garden walk
    Pattered its pretty feet;
And with its head upon her lap
    The little lamb would lay
Asleep beneath the elm-tree's shade,
    Upon the summer's day,
While she twined flowers around its neck,
    And called it her "Sweet May."

THE FAIRY RING.

LET us laugh and let us sing,
Dancing in a merry ring;
We 'll be fairies on the green,
Sporting round the fairy queen.

Like the seasons of the year,
Round we circle in a sphere :
I 'll be summer, you 'll be spring,
Dancing in a fairy ring.

Harry will be winter wild,
Little Charlie, autumn mild ;
Summer, autumn, winter, spring,
Dancing in a fairy ring.

Spring and summer glide away,
Autumn comes with tresses gray,
Winter, hand in hand with spring,
Dancing in a fairy ring.

Faster ! faster ! round we go,
While our cheeks like roses glow.
Free as birds upon the wing,
Dancing in a fairy ring.

ARTHUR'S ROCKING-HORSE.

Do, dear aunt, — do come and see
What dear papa has bought for me ;
Come, now come, — 'tis in the lobby : —
I can ride it, — I can guide it ;
Papa says 'tis " Arthur's Hobby."

Ah, dear aunt, you well may stare, —
My Rocking-horse is standing there ;

And when mounted on him, fairly,
  I can back him, — I can check him,
  Or I make him gallop rarely.

See my foot in stirrup set,
Springing nimbly, up I get,
And, horseman like, I seize the bridle:
  Up I rein him, down constrain him,
  He never wishes to be idle.

Yes, dear Arthur, well you ride,
And mount with grace, 'tis not denied;
I'll name your horse, — "Amazing Bobby."
  Dappled gray, sir, — he's a racer;
Pa' may call him "Arthur's Hobby."

Many ride for riding's sake, —
You as good a journey make;
Theirs the world, and yours the lobby:
  From employment springs enjoyment,
  Romp at home, then, "Arthur's Hobby."

------◆------

THREE LITTLE EGGS.

Here's a nest in the hedge row,
  Half hid by the leaves,
And the sprays, white with blossom,
  Bend o'er it like eaves.

Look in very softly
  Between the green boughs,
While the mother is absent,
  God watches the house.

Straw walls, and a lining
  Of mosses and wool,
Well wrought the small mason,
  His bill all his tool.

Three eggs, blue and speckled,
  Are all it will hold,
But more dear to the mother
  Than diamonds and gold.

She is happy and thankful
  The whole summer long,
With her mate perching near her
  And warbling his song.

God gave them their lodging,
  He gives them their food,
And they trust he will give them
  Whatever is good.

Ah, when your rich blessings,
  ·My child, you forget,

When for some little trouble
  You murmur and fret,

Hear the sweet voices singing
  In hedges and trees,
Will you be less thankful,
  Less trustful than these !

RISING IN THE MORNING.

THRICE welcome to my opening eyes
The morning beam, which bids me rise
  To all the joys of youth ;
For thy protection, whilst I slept,
O Lord, my humble thanks accept,
  And bless my lips with truth.

Like cheerful birds, as I begin
This day, O keep my soul from sin —
  And all things shall be well.
Thou gav'st me health, and clothes, and
    food,
Preserve me innocent and good,
  Till evening curfew bell.

THE CROCODILE.

In the muddy waters
 Of the Hindoo home,
Far beyond our country,
 Does this monster roam.

There he 's worshipped daily,
 By that idol throng,
Where they know no better,
 Than to do this wrong.

Mothers throw their infants
 To his open jaws,
8

Know not they are breaking
   God's eternal laws.

Pray to God, my children,
   When to-night you kneel,
He will to these heathen
   His true Word reveal.

———◆——

BREAKFAST AND PUSS.

HERE's my baby's bread and milk,
For her lip as soft as silk ;
Here 's the basin clean and neat,
Here 's the spoon of silver sweet,
Here 's the stool, and here 's the chair,
For my little lady fair.

No, you must not spill it out,
And drop the bread and milk about ;
But let it stand before you flat,
And pray remember pussy-cat :
Poor old pussy-cat, that purrs,
All so patiently for hers.

True she runs about the house,
Catching now and then a mouse,

But, though she thinks it very nice,
That only makes a tiny slice :
So don't forget that you should stop,
And leave poor puss a little drop.

———◆———

THE GOOD SHEPHERD.

HEAVENLY Shepherd! blest are all
Who have heard thy gracious call,
Whom thou guidest in the way,
Whom thou watchest night and day,
Poor and helpless though they be ;
Blest are all that follow thee.

By the quiet waters led,
In the pleasant pastures fed,
Guarded well from every harm,
Carried on thy faithful arm,
Weak and sinful though they be,
Blest are all that follow thee.

Jesus, Shepherd kind and good,
Thou for me hast shed thy blood ;
Though a little child I am,
In thy flock is many a lamb,
Make me one, and let me be
Ever glad to follow thee.

My weak footsteps gently lead,
Where thy happy flock doth feed,
In thy bosom let me lie,
All my daily wants supply,
Now and ever let me be
Willing, Lord, to follow thee.

———◆———

THE HAND POST.

THE night was dark, the sun was hid
    Beneath the mountain gray:
And not a single star appeared,
    To shoot a silver ray.

Across the path the owlet flew,
    And screamed along the blast,
And onward, with a quickened step,
    Benighted Henry passed.

At intervals, amid the gloom
    A flash of lightning played,
And showed the ruts with water filled,
    And the black hedge's shade.

Again, in thickest darkness plunged
    He groped his way to find;

And now he thought he spied beyond
  A form of horrid kind.

In deadly white it upward rose,
  Of cloak or mantle bare,
And held its naked arms across,
  To catch him by the hair.

Poor Henry felt his blood run cold,
  At what before him stood ;
But well, thought he, no harm, I 'm sure,
  Can happen to the good.

So calling all his courage up,
  He to the goblin went ;
And eager through the dismal gloom
  His piercing eyes he bent.

And when he came well nigh the ghost
  That gave him such affright,
He clapped his hands upon his side,
  And loudly laughed outright.

For 't was a friendly hand-post stood
  His wandering steps to guide ;
And thus he found that to the good
  No evil can betide.

And well, thought he, one thing I 've learnt,
  Nor soon shall I forget,
Whatever frightens me again,
  To march straight up to it.

And when I hear an idle tale
  Of goblins and a ghost,
I 'll tell of this my lonely ride,
  And the tall white Hand Post.

GOING TO BED AT NIGHT.

RECEIVE my body, pretty bed!
Soft pillow, oh, receive my head!
  And thanks, my parents kind,
Those comforts who for me provide;
Their precepts still shall be my guide,
  Their love I 'll keep in mind.

My hours misspent this day I rue,
My good things done, how very few!
  Forgive my fault, O Lord!
This night, if in thy grace I rest,
To-morrow may I rise refreshed,
  To keep thy holy word.

A HUMBLE MIND.

SINCE I am a little child,
Humble I should be, and mild,
Always ready to be taught,
And to do the things I ought.

When I cannot have my way,
I must no ill-will display,
But must learn to bend my will,
And be kind and gentle still.

Pride and anger I must shun,
Nor be rude to any one;

Evil tempers must not rise
To offend God's holy eyes.

Lord, thy grace and help I seek ;
Make me humble, modest, meek ;
Poor in spirit may I be,
And submit myself to thee.

———◆———

COME AND PLAY.

LITTLE sister, come away
And let us in the garden play,
For it is a pleasant day.

On the grass plat let us sit,
Or, if you please, we 'll play a bit,
And run about all over it.

But the fruit we will not pick,
For that would be a naughty trick,
And very likely make us sick.

Nor will we pick the pretty flowers
That grow about the beds and bowers,
Because you know they are not ours.

We 'll take the daisies, white and red,
Because mamma has often said,
That we may gather them instead.

And much I hope we always may
Our very dear mamma obey,
And mind whatever she may say.

———◆———

GREEDY RICHARD.

" I THINK I want some pies this morning,"
Said Dick, stretching himself and yawning ;
So down he,threw his slate and books,
And sauntered to the pastry-cook's.

And there he cast his greedy eyes
Round on the jellies and the pies,
So to select, with anxious care,
The very nicest that was there.

At last the point was thus decided,
As his opinion was divided
'Twixt pie and jelly, he was loth
Either to leave—so took them both.

Now Richard never could be pleased
To eat till hunger was appeased ;

But he 'd go on to cram and stuff,
Long after he had had enough.

I sha'n't take any more," said Dick.
" Dear me, I feel extremely sick,
I cannot eat this other bit ;
I wish I had not tasted it."

Then slowly rising from his seat,
He threw the cheesecake in the street,
And left the tempting pastry-cook's
With very discontented looks.

Just then a man with wooden leg
Met Dick, and held his hat to beg :
And while he told his mournful case,
Looked at him with imploring face.

Dick, wishing to relieve his pain,
His pockets searched, but searched in vain,
And so at last he did declare
He had not got a farthing there.

The beggar turned with face of grief,
And look of patient unbelief,
While Richard, now completely tamed,
Felt inconceivably ashamed.

" I wish," said he (but wishing's vain),
" I 'd got my money back again,
And had not spent my last, to pay
For what I only threw away.

"Another time I 'll take advice,
And not buy things because they 're nice,
But rather save my little store
To give poor folks who want it more."

———◆———

IDLE MARY.

OH, Mary, this will never do !
    This work is sadly done, my dear,
And then so little of it too !
    You have not taken pains, I fear.

Oh no, your work has been forgotten,
    Indeed you 've hardly thought of *that;*
I saw you roll your ball of cotton
    About the floor to please the cat.

See, here are stitches straggling wide,
    And others reaching down so far ;
I 'm very sure you have not tried
    In this, at least, to please mamma.

The little girl who will not sew,
  Must neither be allowed to play;
And then I hope, my love, that you
  Will take more pains another day.

———◆———

THE FROLICSOME KITTEN.

DEAR kitten, do lie still, I say,
  I really want you to be quiet,
Instead of scampering away
  And always making such a riot.

There, only see! you've torn my frock,
  And poor mamma must put a patch in;
I'll give you a right earnest knock,
  To cure you of the trick of scratching.

Nay, do not scold your little cat,
  She does not know what 'tis you're say-
    ing;
And every time you give a pat,
  She thinks you mean it all for playing.

But if poor pussy understood
  The lesson that you want to teach her,
And did not choose to be so good,
  She'd be, indeed, a naughty creature.

THE HOOP.

LIKE a bird upon the bough,
When the summer breezes blow,
And the woods with music ring,
Merrily, merrily voices sing.

School is closed and tasks are done,
Flowers are laughing in the sun,
Like the songsters of the air,
Pretty ladies, banish care!

Roll away! how safe it goes!
Cheeks are glowing like the rose,
Health and joy our pastimes bring,
Merrily, merrily our voices ring.

Liberty makes labor sweet,
Toil is followed by a treat,
Tasks have purchased joy and play,
And the summer holiday.

Roll away and never fear,
Gladness only enters here;
Free from care we'll laugh and sing,
Merrily, merrily voices ring!

———◆———

PRECOCIOUS PIGGY.

WHERE are you going to, you little pig?
"I'm leaving my mother, I'm growing so
　　　big!"
　　So big, young pig,
　　So young, so big!
What, leaving your mother, you foolish young
　　　pig!

Where are you going to, you little pig?
"I've got a new spade, and I'm going to
　　　dig!"
　　To dig, little pig!
　　A little pig dig!
Well, I never saw a pig with a spade that could
　　　dig!

Where are you going to, you little pig?
" Why, I 'm going to have a nice ride in a
        gig! "
        In a gig, little pig!
        What, a pig in a gig!
Well, I never yet saw a pig ride in a gig!

Where are you going to, you little pig?
" Well, I 'm going to the Queen's Head to
        have a nice swig! "
        A swig, little pig!
        A pig have a swig!
What, a pig at the Queen's Head, having a
        swig!

Where are you going to, you little pig?
" Why, I 'm going to the ball to dance a fine
        jig! "
        A jig, little pig!
        A pig dance a jig!
Well, I never before saw a pig dance a jig!

Where are you going to, you little pig?
" I 'm going to the Fair to run a fine rig! "
        A rig, little pig!
        A pig run a rig!
Well, I never before saw a pig run a rig!

Where are you going to, you little pig!
" I 'm going to the barber's to buy me a wig ! "
        A wig, little pig!
        A pig in a wig!
Why, who ever before saw a pig in a wig?

Where are you going to, you little pig?
" The butcher is coming, I 've grown so big ! "
        The butcher !   Poor pig !
        Are you grown so big ?
Well, I think it high time then you hop the
        twig!

———◆———

THE RAINBOW.

THE rain is nearly over,
    And bright'ning comes the sun,
And from their leafy shelter
    The birds hop one by one.

Their chirping voices calling,
    I think, each has to say
The Rainbow, see how brilliant
    Its colors are, and gay.

On rain-wet sprays alighting,
    They shake the pendant drops,

As if each knew they sparkle,
    And glitter, as he hops.

Such beads of shining water
    From that rich painted Bow.
The sunbeams on them falling,
    Produce the varied glow.

Then, thinking on its promise,
    Admiring let us view,
There, blended in the Rainbow,
    Bright nature's every hue.

EARLY RISING.

"I LIKE to rise early, Louisa," said Jane,—
    " And wake, in the summer, by five ;
Then with dearest papa, I walk up the lane,
    E'er the bee sallies forth from its hive.

" I have learnt of papa, to think that the day,
    Like a book, should be properly read,
But ill it's perused, — the first page thrown
      away, —
    By thoughtlessly lying in bed.

9

" To see the sun rise, — what an exquisite
    treat,
The sky wearing a mantle of gold,
And the birds chirping loud, and the air smell
    ing sweet, —
The half, dear, can never be told.

" All then look so fresh, — the fields and the
    sky, —
E'en the sun in the morning looks new; —
'Tis pleasant to watch, before it is high,
    How it raises the night-veil of dew.

" Papa then directs me to look at each flower,
    And tells me their uses besides ; —
Oh, I love to rise early, and love at that hour
    To learn from so truthful a guide."

THE BETTER LAND.

WHITHER, pilgrims, are you going
    Each with staff in hand ?
We are going on a journey
    At the King's command.

Over plains, and hills, and valleys,
We are going to His palace
   In the better land.

Fear ye not the way so lonely,
   You, a feeble band ?
No, for friends unseen are near us,
   Angels round us stand.
Christ, our leader, walks beside us,
He will guard us, — He will guide us
   To the better land.

Tell me, pilgrims, what you hope for
   In the better land ?
Spotless robes and crowns of glory
   From a Saviour's hand.
We shall drink of Life's clear river,
We shall dwell with God forever,
   In the better land.

Will you let me travel with you
   To the better land?
Come away — we bid you welcome
   To our little band.
Come, O come ! we cannot leave you,
Christ is waiting to receive you
   In the better land.

FOR THE LORD'S DAY MORNING.

THIS is the day when Christ arose
    So early from the dead:
Why should I keep my eyelids closed,
    And waste my hours in bed?

This is the day when Jesus broke
    The power of death and hell:
And shall I still wear Satan's yoke,
    And love my sins so well?

To-day with pleasure Christians meet,
    To pray and hear thy word;
And I will go with cheerful feet,
    To learn thy will, O Lord.

I'll leave my sport to read and pray,
    And so prepare for heaven :
Oh may I love this blessed day,
    The best of all the seven !

THE KIND MAMMA.

COME, dear, and sit upon my knee,
And give me kisses, one, two, three,
And tell me whether you love me,
                        My baby.

For this I'm sure, that I love you,
And many, many things I do,
And all day long I sit and sew
                        For baby.

And then at night I lie awake,
Thinking of things that I can make,
And trouble that I mean to take,
                        For baby.

And when you're good and do not cry,
Nor into naughty passions fly,
You can't think how papa and I
                        Love baby.

But if my little girl should grow
To be a naughty child, you know,
'T would grieve mamma to see her so,
               My baby.

And when you saw me pale and thin,
By grieving for my baby's sin,
I think you 'd wish that you had been
               A better baby!

THE FROG WHO WOULD A WOOING GO.

THERE was a frog lived in a well,
And a merry mouse lived in a mill.

This froggy would a wooing go,
But could n't walk for the corn on his toe.

So he mounted, and away did ride,
With a sword and a pistol by his side.

He rode till he came to Miss Mouse's hall,
And then he did both knock and call.

"Pray, Miss Mouse, are you within?"
"Oh, yes, kind sir, and going to spin."

" Pray, Miss Mouse, will you marriage make,
With a young frog that's tall and straight ? "

" My uncle Rat went out this morn,
And I won't consent till his return."

Her uncle Rat he did come home,
Saying, " Who's been here since I've been
     gone ? "

" There's been a noble, tall, straight man,
Who vows he 'll marry me if he can."

" We 'll have the wedding in the mill."
" Oh yes, kind uncle, so we will."

Now while they all at dinner sat,
In came the kitten and the cat.

The cat seized uncle Rat by the crown,
The kitten pulled the poor wife down.

The mouse she did run up the wall,
And said, " Oh dear ! they 'll kill us all."

The frog he did run up the brook,
And there he met a hungry duck.

The Juck he swallowed her down his
    throat,
Saying, "There's an end of these fine
    folk."

—◆—

THE WAY TO BE HAPPY.

How pleasant it is, at the end of the day,
    No follies to have to repent!
But reflect on the past, and be able to say,
    That my time has been properly spent.

When I've done all my business with patience
    and care,
    And been good, and obliging, and kind;
I lie on my pillow, and sleep away there,
    With a happy and peaceable mind.

But instead of all this, when it must be con-
    fessed
    That I careless and idle have been,
I lie down as usual and go to my rest,
    But feel discontented within.

Then as I don't like all the trouble I've had,
    In future I'll try to prevent it;
For I never am naughty without being sad,
    Or good — without being contented.

THE WAVES ON THE SEA-SHORE.

ROLL on, roll on, you restless waves,
    That toss about and roar ;
Why do you all run back again
    When you have reached the shore ?

Roll on, roll on, you noisy waves,
    Roll higher up the strand ;

How is it that you cannot pass
    That line of yellow sand?

Make haste, or else the tide will turn;
    Make haste, you noisy sea;
Roll quite across the bank, and then
    Far on across the lea.

" We must not dare," the waves reply:
    " That line of yellow sand
Is laid along the shore to bound
    The waters and the land;

" And all should keep to time and place,
    And all should keep to rule,
Both waves upon the sandy shore,
    And little boys at school."

ABOUT LEARNING TO READ.

HERE's a gay pretty book, full of verses to
        sing,
But Lucy can't read it; oh, what a sad thing!
And such funny stories, — with pictures, too,
        — look:
I am glad I can read such a beautiful book.

But come, little Lucy, now what do you say,
Shall I begin teaching you pretty great A ?
And then all the letters that stand in a row ?
That you may be able to read it, you know ?

A great many children have no kind mamma
To teach them to read, and poor children they
      are ;
But Lucy shall learn all her letters to tell,
And I hope by and by, she will read very
      well.

MISTER FOX.

A Fox went out in a hungry plight,
And he begged of the moon to give him light,
For he'd many miles to trot that night,
    Before he could reach his den O !

And first he came to a farmer's yard,
Where the ducks and geese declared it hard
That their nerves should be shaken, and their
    rest be marred,
    By the visit of Mister Fox O !

He took the gray goose by the sleeve ;
Says he, " Madam goose, and by your leave,
I 'll take you away without reprieve,
    And carry you home to my den O'! "

'He seized the black duck by the neck,
And swung her all across his back.
The black duck cried out " Quack ! quack !
    quack ! "
    With her legs hanging dangling down O !

Then old Mrs. Slipper-slopper jumped out of
    bed,
, And out of the window she popped her head, —
" John, John, John, the gray goose is gone,
    And the fox is off to his den O ! "

Then John he went up to the hill,
And he blew a blast both loud and shrill ;
Says the fox, " This is very pretty music —
    still
    I 'd rather be at my den O ! "

At last the fox got home to his den ;
To his dear little foxes, eight, nine, ten,
Says he, " You 're in luck, here 's a good fat
    duck,
With her legs hanging dangling down O ! "

He then sat down with his hungry wife ;
They did very well without fork or knife ;
·They never ate a better goose in all their life,
   And the little ones picked the bones O ! ''

BEFORE MY·BROTHER WENT TO SEA

WE did not mind the winters then,
   Nor care how loud the wind might blow ;
The snow might fall, and freeze again,
   The lowering clouds might come and go ;
Our home was blithe, our hearts were free,
Before my brother went to sea.

But now my mother's cheek grows white
   To hear the rising of the blast ;
My father's look has lost its light,
   And slow the stormy months go past.
Things are not as they used to be,
Before my brother went to sea.

Yet, though the ocean wastes be wide,
   I know that Providence is there ;
Nor can the winds and waves divide
   Our absent from His ceaseless care.
Therefore, at times, it seems to me,
'' My brother will come safe from sea.''

SISTER MARY AND BROTHER JOHN.

THEY had one seat in a mossy nook,
They learned their lessons from one old book,
And played together by lane and brook.

At home or abroad, in house or lawn,
When holidays reigned, or school came on,
'Twas " Sister Mary and Brother John."

They feared not the sun that made them brown,
They cared not for winter's frosty frown,
Nor minded how fast the rain came down.

Parting was all their fear and dread;
Father and mother both were dead,
And left them little, the neighbors said.

But Mary and John had laid a scheme
For future days when their fortune came,
And they were playing the grown up game.

They would have a cottage of their own,
With roses, and woodbine overgrown,
And the largest fig-tree ever known.

There they would live their whole lives through,
And watch how the figs and roses grew;
I wonder if it all came true!

For far from our village they have gone,
And none can tell us how things go on
With " Sister Mary and Brother John."

———◆———

THE MOUSE WITH A BELL.

.   In a large house, some mice, —
    And I might say a number, —
    Nibbled all that was nice,
    And disturbed people's slumber.

For, at night, their sharp teeth,
   All to get at cook's larder,
Were heard gnawing beneath
   The deal floor, — or wood harder.

Well, — the cook checked her rage,
   And considered a minute ;
Then she set a trap-cage,
   And soon caught a mouse in it.

" Now," said she, " my young thief, —
   This bright bell, so adorning,
You shall wear like a chief,
   To give other rogues warning."

'Twas then tied round his neck,
   And away in a twink'ling,
Mousy ran, — nor looked back,
   Perhaps pleased with its tink'ling.

The house soon became clear
   Of the mice, — for none tarried,
The sweet music to hear,
   That their proud brother carried.

Cookey thus freed the house,
   But, it may be ne'er pondered,

As did the poor mouse,
  The while lonely he wandered.

" Ah," he said, " pride, I see,
  Wins no joy for its owner;
For, my friends — how they flee,
  Leaving me a sâd moaner."

As he spoke, — lo! a jink! —
  'T was the bell, from its tying,
Coming loose at a link,
  There before him was lying.

Mousy gave a great leap,
  And said, all in a twitter,
" There, far from me keep,
  With your music and glitter.

" For my friends, now, I'll look, —
  Again free from your clatter:
But respects to the cook, —
  Should you ever get at her."

Polite mousy was he
  To the lady who caught him;
And was grateful, may be,
  For the lesson so taught him.
          10

THE FAITHFUL DOG.

A LITTLE boy, one summer day,
Went out into the fields to play;
And, pleased, he wandered far and wide,
With faithful Rover by his side.

"But," said he, "I should like to go
To some clear brook, where lilies grow;"
And so his flowers away he threw,
Though many were of lovely hue.

The water gained, — right glad was he
Such beauteous lily-cups to see;
To the green banks he quickly ran,
And soon to gather them began.

But, ah! — how sad the tale to tell, —
He missed his step, and in he fell,

And gliding from the sloping bank,
Screamed loud and sadly e'er he sank.

Then Rover, plunging from the shore,
Back to the land his master bore,
Wet, but not hurt, — the little boy
Now cried, while Rover barked forth joy.

THE BUTTERFLY.

THE butterfly's an idle thing,
Nor honey makes, nor yet can sing,
　　Like to the bee and bird ;
Nor does it, like the prudent ant,
Lay up the grain for time of want,
　　A wise and cautious hoard.

My youth is but a summer's day,
Then, like the bee and ant, I'll lay
　　A store of learning by ;
And though from flower to flower I rove,
My stock of wisdom I'll improve,
　　Nor be a Butterfly.

MY FATHER'S HOUSE UPON THE HILL.

Its white walls glisten through the trees,
   Its windows catch the sunset's glow,
Its rising smoke the traveller sees
   From the broad river's banks below.

There 's peace around it day and night,
   And love that makes a summer still;
Through all the year keeps warm and bright
   My father's house upon the hill.

In pinching times the poor come there
From many a hut and hamlet round ;
For ready help and kindly cheer,
Within its doors are always found.

Our land has halls where plenty flows,
Has lords and squires, with wealth at will ;
But best of all the poor man knows
My father's house upon the hill.

In week-day work, and Sabbath rest,
The passing seasons o'er it glide,
With many a game, and many a guest,
At harvest-home, and Christmas tide.

Flowers grow without, and smiles within,
The hearth is never sad or chill ;
Lord, keep from grief and save from sin,
My father's house upon the hill.

THE LITTLE BEGGAR GIRL.

THERE 's a poor beggar going by,
I see her looking in :
She 's just about as big as I,
Only so very thin.

She has no shoes upon her feet,
　She is so very poor:
And hardly any thing to eat;
　I pity her, I'm sure.

But I have got nice clothes, you know,
　And meat, and bread, and fire;
And dear mamma, that loves me so,
　And all that I desire.

If I were forced to stroll so far,
　Oh dear, what should I do?
I wish she had a kind mamma,
　Just such a one as you.

Here, little girl, come back again,
　And hold that ragged hat,
And I will put a penny in, —
　There, buy some bread with that.

———◆———

CONTENTED JOHN.

ONE honest John Tompkins, a hedger and
　　ditcher,
Although he was poor, did not want to be
　　richer;

For all such vain wishes to him were pre-
    vented
By a fortunate habit of being contented.

Though cold was the weather, or dear was the
    food,
John never was found in a murmuring mood;
For this he was constantly heard to declare,
What he could not prevent he would cheer-
    fully bear.

For why should I grumble and murmur? he
    said:
If I cannot get meat, I can surely get bread;
And though fretting may make my calamities
    deeper,
It never can make bread and cheese any
    cheaper.

If John was afflicted with sickness or pain,
He wished himself better, but did not com-
    plain;
Nor lie down to fret, in despondence and sor-
    row,
But said—that he hoped to be better to-
    morrow.

If any one wronged him, or treated him ill,
Why John was good-natured and sociable still;
For he said — that revenging the injury done,
Would be making two rogues, where there
    need be but one.

And thus honest John, though his station was
    humble,
Passed through this sad world without even a
    grumble;
And I wish that some folks who are greater
    and richer,
Would copy John Tompkins, the hedger and
    ditcher.

———◆———

QUESTIONS AND ANSWERS.

Who showed the little ant the way
    Her narrow hole to bore,
And spend the pleasant summer day,
    In laying up her store?

The sparrow builds her clever nest
    Of wool, and hay, and moss;
Who told her how to build it best,
    And lay the twigs across?

Who taught the busy bee to fly
    Among the sweetest flowers,

And lay his store of honey by,
　　To eat in winter hours!

'T was God who showed them all the way,
　　And gave their little skill,
And teaches children, if they pray,
　　To do His holy will.

———◆———

OUR LITTLE ROSE.

How early she went from our hearth and our
　　play,
The youngest of all, yet the first called away,
　　And oh, but the sorrow was sore!
No losses nor partings till then had we seen;
No discord, no changes among us had been;
　　No death in our dwelling before.

At times we are weary and sad for her yet;
I know that my mother will never forget.
   She says it is sinful to grieve ;
But we miss the blithe tone, and we miss the
      bright face,
And her seat by the fire is a sorrowful place,
   At the fall of the dark winter eve.

For now in the churchyard our hearts have a
      share ;
Since over the sleep of our young sister there,
   The grass of the summer-time grows.
But have we not learned that a better home
      lies
Above the green grave, and above the blue
      skies,
   And there we'll meet our little Rose.

THE TRUE FRIEND.

CHILDREN, you have heard the story
How the Lord of life and glory
Left his Father's house on high
And came down to earth to die.
   To a friend so true and tender
   What should you not freely render ?

When his suffering here was ended,
He to heaven again ascended,
Now he reigns in glory there,
Yet he loves to hear your prayer.
To a friend so true and tender
Who would not all praises render?

This good Saviour loveth dearly
Those like you who seek him early,
There is none too young to sin,
None too young his grace to win.
To this friend so true and tender
Will you not your heart surrender?

Choose this friend, ye poor and friendless,
Trust his love so deep and endless,
It will bless you all your days
And your souls to glory raise.
Children, to this friend so tender,
Now, O now! your heart surrender.

———◆———

CREATION.

Come, child, look upward to the sky,
    Behold the sun and moon,
The expanse of stars that sparkle high
    To cheer the midnight gloom.

Come, child, and now behold the earth
  In varied beauty stand;
The product view of six days' birth,
  How wondrous and how grand!

The fields, the meadows, and the plain,
  The little laughing hills,
The waters too, the mighty main,
  The rivers and the rills.

Come then, behold them all, and say,
  "How came these things to be
That stand before, whichever way
  I turn myself to see?"

'T was God, who made the earth and sea,
  To whom the angels bow;
'T was God, who made both thee and me,
  The God who sees us now.

—◆—

THE PLAY HOUR.

THE bell has rung; with merry shout,
From school the boys are rushing out;
Now books are closed, with what delight
They grasp the marbles, ball, and kite.

Shout on, light hearts! one loves to hear
This burst of voices fresh and clear.
To watch a troop of schoolboys gay
Enjoy like you the hour of play.

How short it seems! yet to the boy
Its shortness brings a keener joy,
The hours of work that go before
Endear the hour of leisure more.

Shout on, glad hearts! in boyhood learn
Your pleasure through your toil to earn ;
If life were all one idle day
You would not prize the hour of play.

Improve the golden hours that bring
Such stores of knowledge on the wing,
None have used them well but knew
That labor's path is pleasure's too.

Choose heavenly wisdom as your guide,
And peace will follow at her side.
A purer joy bless manhood's way
Than brightened boyhood's hour of play.

THE IMITATOR.

AN arrow from a bow just shot,
Flew upwards to heaven's canopy
And cried, with pompous self-conceit,
To the King Eagle scornfully : —
" Look here — I can as high as thou,
And, towards the sun, even higher sail!"
The Eagle smiled and said, " Oh, fool,
What do thy borrowed plumes avail?
By others' strength thou dost ascend,
But by thyself dost downward tend."

From the German.

THE YOUNG CARPENTER.

Whene'er his father would permit,
  Young Jemmy to the workshop hied;
And there he quietly would sit,
  With nails and hammer by his side.

Ah, youthful Jem, — the time will come,
  When thou wilt have to labor hard;
Then whilst, my boy, thou art at home,
  May nought thy aim to work retard.

When first his father let him saw, —
  What pleasure sparkled in his eye;
And in the fence when stopped a flaw,
  The piece held fast, — though nailed awry.

To work thus kindly led, — the son
  His father's best of aid became,-
And all who wished a job well done
  Were sure to mention Jemmy's name.

——◆——

THREE LITTLE KITTENS.

Three little kittens they lost their mittens,
And they began to cry,

"Oh! mammy dear,
We sadly fear,
Our mittens we have lost!"
"What! lost your mittens,
You naughty kittens,
Then you shall have no pie."
Miew, miew, miew, miew,
Miew, miew, miew, miew. ·

The three little kittens they found their mit-
tens,
And they began to cry,
"Oh! mammy dear,
See here, see here,
Our mittens we have found."
"What! found your mittens,
You little kittens,
Then you shall have some pie."
Purr, purr, purr, purr,
Purr, purr, purr, purr.

The three little kittens put on their mittens,
And soon ate up the pie;
"Oh! mammy dear,
We greatly fear,
Our mittens we have soiled."

—" What! soiled your mittens,
  You naughty kittens! "
        Then they began to sigh,
            Miew, miew, miew, miew,
            Miew, miew, miew, miew.

The three little kittens they washed their
      mittens,
And hung them up to dry;
        " Oh! mammy dear,
        Look here, look here,
        Our mittens we have washed."
" What! washed your mittens,
  You darling kittens!
        But I smell a rat close by!
            Hush! hush!" Miew, miew,
            Miew, miew, miew, m̤ew.

11

OUR COUSINS FAR OFF IN THE WEST.

' T is long since we bid them farewell,
    One morning, with blessings and tears,
Their farm at the foot of the fell,
    A stranger has tilled it for years.
Beyond the wide sea is their home;
    Yet still we remember them best,
And welcome the letters that come
    From our cousins far off in the west.

They tell us of forests and floods,
    With names never heard on our shore,
Of towns growing up, where the woods
    Had waved but the summer before;

Of churches and homes like our own,
  Where families labor and rest,
No strangers to us have they grown,
  Our cousins far off in the west.

———◆———

THE NINE BROTHERS.

NINE brothers there are,
All known near and far,
And to you, — or you 're sadly to blame :
  They help all who ask, —
  To them easy task, —
Now, before you I'll call them by name.

You 'll know them at once,
Unless you 're a dunce : —
See, here they come, — 1, 2, 3, and
  Yes, — 4, 5, and 6, —
  This order we fix, —
And 7, 8, 9, now you see.

Rare deeds do these nine,
For when they combine,
By ADDITION, the total they say ;
  Then again, if need be,
  At times they agree,
To SUBTRACT, — or a part take away.

Oh, funny nine boys!—
When they're tired of toys,
By Multiplication they make
A large sum,—and the whole
Of the lines look quite droll,
In the sloping direction they take.

Sometimes when play's o'er,
They try one rule more,
Division,—with each other's aid;
And by it they say
How many fives may
Of fifty or twenty be made.

A companion is theirs,
Who frequently shares
Their wealth,—having none of his own;
Cipher Nought (0) is his name,
And by it he came
Because he is nothing, alone.

Act well,—for these chaps
Show people's mishaps;
Of their power, then, let us beware;
For should we, some day,
Owe what we can't pay,
They'll know it,—so let us take care.

THE SCHOOL.

A WILLING little scholar
    Into your school I bring;
Oh, make him welcome, master,
    And teach him every thing.

Teach him a little reading,
    A little writing too;
And teach him how his little sums
    Full quickly he may do.

And teach him to obey you,
    And to be just and true;
To know the truth from falsehood,
    And speak it boldly too.

And teach him, O, good master!
Whatever may befall,
To love his God, and trust him;
For that is more than all.

THE SEVEN BIRTHDAYS.

WE had seven birthdays in the year;
We kept them all with merry cheer,
For father, mother, and sisters three,
For brother Alfred, and for me.

Some came round with the winter's snows,
Some with midsummer, and the rose,
Some at the time when brown leaves fall,
But there were games and gifts for all.

Father's was kept with home-brewed ale,
Mother's was kept with talk and tale,
Sisters' were kept with frills and frocks,
Alfred's and mine with woodland walks.

'T is long ago, and the churchyard yew
Bends o'er father and mother too;
Brother and sisters all have grown
To troubles, and houses of their own.

The years are busy — the world is wide —
We have scattered far from the old fireside ;
Some mind the ledger, some mind the plough,
But where are the seven brave birthdays now ?

DAME DUCK'S LECTURE.

OLD Mother Duck has hatched a brood
    Of ducklings, small and callow :
Their little wings are short, their down
    Is mottled gray and yellow.

There is a quiet little stream,
    That runs into the moat,
Where tall green sedges spread their leaves,
    And water-lilies float.

Close by the margin of the brook
    The old duck made her nest,
Of straw, and leaves, and withered grass,
    And down from her own breast.

And there she sat for four long weeks,
    In rainy days and fine,
Until the ducklings all came out —
    Four, five, six, seven, eight, nine.

One peeped out from beneath her wing,
  One scrambled on her back;
" That's very rude," said old Dame Duck,
  " Get off! quack, quack, quack, quack ! "

" 'T is close," said Dame Duck, shoving out
  The egg-shells with her bill,
" Besides, it never suits young ducks
  To keep them sitting still."

So, rising from her nest, she said,
  " Now, children, look at me :
A well-bred duck should waddle so,
  From side to side — d'ye see ? "

" Yes," said the little ones, and then
  She went on to explain :
" A well-bred duck turns in its toes
  As I do — try again."

" Yes," said the ducklings, waddling on;
  " That's better," said their mother;
" But well-bred ducks walk in a row,
  Straight — one behind another."

" Yes," said the little ducks again,
  All waddling in a row :

" Now to the pond," said old Dame Duck —
   Splash, splash, and in they go.

" Let me swim first," said old Dame Duck —
   " To this side, now to that;
There, snap at those great brown-winged flies,
   They make young ducklings fat.

" Now when you reach the poultry-yard,
   The hen-wife, Molly Head,
Will feed you, with the other fowls,
   On bran and mashed-up bread;

" The hens will peck and fight, but mind,
   I hope that all of you
Will gobble up the food as fast
   As well-bred ducks should do.

" You 'd better get into the dish,
   Unless it is too small;
In that case, I should use my foot,
   And overturn it all."

The ducklings did as they were bid,
   And found the plan so good,
That, from that day, the other fowls,
   Got hardly any food.

SOPHY'S NEW BABY BROTHER.

Ah, nurse, you really are too bad,
Not before now, to say I had
A baby brother come to live
With us, and so much pleasure give.

How did I find it out at last,
Let's see, — but up I 've come so fast,
That really, now I do not know;
But, come, the baby to me show.

Oh! what a darling, darling prize!
With little cheeks, and nose, and eyes;
I say, eyes, though they 're shut, — but you,
Dear nurse, have seen them, are they blue?

One kiss, I surely, nurse, may take;
Ah, see, that touch has made him wake;
His hands are raised above his head,
With fingers closed, — and now they 're
        spread.

Just look, how small they are to mine,
And with what pinky white they shine;

To work they never must be taught,
But still that is a silly thought.

Hands are to use, — and these may be
As rough as Ben's, who goes to sea:
Ah, well, I love them now, and when
Grown hard and brown, I'll love them then.

And now it comes into my head,
That I have heard it sometime said,
People oft take unhappy ways,
From what they see in childhood's days.

Then now's the time for me to prove
That I my baby brother love, — ·
So pretty is he, 't would be sad,
Were he to get a temper bad.

So, nurse, if ever I forget,
And, pettish bad example set,
These words from you pray let me hear,
" Think how you loved the baby, dear."

Your finger's raised, it means, I know,
That it is time for me to go ;
Before the baby wakes and cries ;
Another time I'll see his eyes.

THE WOODCUTTER.

THE Woodcutter, tottering under his load,
　　Comes tired from the wood to his home ;
His dog trotting by him beguiles the rough
　　　　road,
　　So glad with his master to roam.

Though hardship and toil be the Woodcutter's
　　　　lot,
　　He heeds not the world or its frown,
But sleeps as secure with his dog in his cot
　　As the rich on their pillows of down.

He rises as gay as the lark in the morn,
　　His little dog barking so glad ,
And though that his raiment be homely and
　　　　torn,
　　His heart is not heavy or sad.

With honest exertion from morning till night
　　He patiently toils for his bread ;
His wants are so few and his purse is so light
　　That care never cumbers his head.

WHEN MY MOTHER WAS HERE.

WE have not grown poor, and we have not
    grown cross;
But our days have a chill, and our memories
    a loss;
The fireside looks lonely, the table looks bare,
Though all sit around with enough and to
    spare.

My father comes home at the fall of night,
His step has grown weary, his hair has grown
      white;
He smiles on us yet, but his smile has no
      cheer,
It never was so when my mother was here.

Now no one looks out when we go to the
      school,
Or warns us to keep from the ice on the pool;
And no one comes softly to see how we sleep,
When the night hours are dark, and the silence
      is deep.

Together we go on the long summer walk,
But nobody cheers it with stories and talk;
We gather the blossoms from bank and from
      bough,
But nobody welcomes us home with them
      now.

We read her old Bible; we have not forgot
The hymns that she loved, and the prayers
      that she taught;
Our love is still kindly, our home is still dear,
But not what they were when my mother was
      here.

WASHING AND DRESSING.

Ah, why will my dear little girl be so cross,
    And cry, and look sulky, and pout?
To lose her sweet smile is a terrible loss,
    I can't even kiss her without.

You say, you don't like to be washed and
    be drest;
    But would you be dirty and foul?
Come, drive that long sob from your dear little
    breast,
    And clear your sweet face from its scowl.

If the water is cold, and the comb hurts your
    head,
    And the soap has got into your eye,
Will the water grow warmer for all that you've
    said,
    And what good will it do you to cry?

It is not to tease you, and hurt you, my sweet,
    But only for kindness and care,
That I wash you, and dress you, and make
    you look neat,
    And comb out your tanglesome hair.

I don't mind the trouble, if you would not
    cry,
But pay me for all with a kiss.
That's right, take the towel, and wipe your
    wet eye,
    I thought you'd be good after this.

———◆———

PATIENT PATTY.

WHY, little baby, — again and again,
Must I jog you, and jog you in vain?
    Really, really I thought you asleep:
Pussy-cat sleeps, little baby, without
All this singing, and jogging, and rout,
    Rolled up, round-about-round, in a heap.
Sing then, ho, — once again, lull-a-bye,
Ah, there, — now you are closing your eye,
    And still as a mouse I will keep.

Patient Patty it was singing so,
And further than this, you must know,
    She was patient by nature and name;
And if she heard any one huff
A baby, — she said " 't was enough
    To make it bad tempered, the same."

AGAIST IDLENESS AND MISCHIEF.

How doth the little busy Bee
  Improve each shining hour,
And gather honey all the day
  From every opening flower!

How skilfully she builds her cell!
  How neat she spreads her wax!
And labors hard to store it well
  With the sweet food she makes.

In works of labor or of skill,
  I would be busy too;
12

For Satan finds some mischief still
   For idle hands to do.

In books, or works, or healthful play,
   Let my first years be past;
That I may give for every day
   Some good account at last.

—◆—

THE FOX AND GEESE.

SOME Geese on a common were feeding,
And naught but their appetite heeding;
The fresh breeze made them hungry no doubt.

Sly Reynard the Fox saw the party,
He, also, could eat very hearty;
But for no meal of grass he looked out.

So quick from the hedge he came bouncing,
And upon a young gosling pouncing
By the neck, bore it nimbly away.

Then a Goose when the mischief was over,
Said, "Friends, when you feed upon clover,
See no danger is near you, I pray."

THE CHATTERBOX.

FROM morning till night it was Lucy's delight
To chatter and talk without stopping;
There was not a day but she rattled away,
Like water forever a dropping!

As soon as she rose, while she put on her
clothes
'T was vain to endeavor to still her;
Nor once did she lack to continue her clack,
Till again she lay down on her pillow.

You 'll think now, perhaps, there would have
been gaps,
If she had n't been wonderful clever;
That her sense was so great, and so witty her
pate,
That it would be forthcoming forever.

But that 's quite absurd, for have you not
heard,
Much tongue and few brains are connected,
That they are supposed to think least who talk
most,
And their wisdom is always suspected?

While Lucy was young, had she bridled her
    tongue
With a little good sense and exertion,
Who knows but she might now have been our
    delight,
Instead of our jest and aversion ?

———◆———

AWAY! AWAY!

AWAY! away! thou little steed,
    Dashing o'er the road so stony,
Fleeter than the zephyr's speed,—
    Bound away, thou gallant pony!

Light's the burden on thy back,
    Fairer load thou could'st not carry;
Curb nor rein thy speed will slack,
    Bit nor bridle bid thee tarry.

Surely both have lost their wits!
    Pretty horse and pretty rider;
Yet with such a grace she sits,
    Nothing evil can betide her.

Faultless both of wind and limb,
    Sure of foot, and always ready,
Where's the horse so proud as him,
    When he bears his handsome lady!

THE ROBBER KITTEN.

A KITTEN once to its mother said,
 " I 'll never more be good,
But I 'll go and be a robber fierce,
 And live in a dreary wood ;
 Wood, wood, wood,
 And live in a dreary wood ! "

So off it went to the dreary wood,
 And there it met a cock,
And blew its head, with a pistol, off,
 Which gave it an awful shock !
 Shock, shock, shock,
 Which gave it an awful shock !

Soon after that it met a cat:
 " Now, give to me your purse,
Or I 'll shoot you through, and stab you too,
 And kill you, which is worse !
 Worse, worse, worse,
 And kill you, which is worse ! "

It climbed a tree to rob a nest
 Of young and tender owls ;

But the branch broke off and the kitten fell,
   With six tremendous howls!
        Howls, howls, howls,
   With six tremendous howls!

One day it met a Robber Dog,
   And they sat down to drink;
The dog did joke, and laugh, and sing,
   Which made the kitten wink!
        Wink, wink, wink,
   Which made the kitten wink!

At last they quarrelled; then they fought,
   Beneath the greenwood tree,
Till puss was felled with an awful club,
   Most terrible to see!
        See, see, see,
   Most terrible to see!

When puss got up, its eye was shut,
   And swelled, and black, and blue;
Moreover, all its bones were sore,
   So it began to mew!
        Mew, mew, mew,
   So it began to mew!

Then up it rose, and scratched its nose,
   And went home very sad;

" Oh, mother dear, behold me here,
   I 'll never more be bad,
      Bad, bad, bad,
   I 'll never more be bad ! "

A PLEASANT SAIL.

THE boat is trimmed with sail and oar,
And all prepared to leave the shore ;
When off we 'll go with wind and tide,
Over the sunny waves to glide.

By headland bold and winding bay,
That look so lovely far away,
How pleasantly we 'll sail along,
And listen to the boatman's song.

When waves are rough and winds are high,
And tempests rage o'er sea and sky,
I would not like the stormy sea, —
Then home and fireside joys for me.

Though tempests rage and billows roar,
God reigns supreme o'er sea and shore,
And shields by his almighty hand,
From dangers both by sea and land.

SULKING.

WHY is Mary standing there,
Leaning down upon a chair,
With such an angry lip and brow?
I wonder what's the matter now.

Come here, my dear, and tell me true,
Is it because I spoke to you
About the work you 've done so slow,
That you are standing fretting so?

Why, then, indeed, I 'm grieved to see
That you can so ill-tempered be.
You make your fault a great deal worse,
By being angry and perverse.

Oh, how much better 't would appear
To see you shed a humble tear,
And then to hear you meekly say,
"I 'll not do so another day."

For you to stand and look so cross,
(Which makes your fault so much the worse)
Is far more naughty, dear, you know,
Than having done your work too slow!

THE SLY OLD FOX.

AWAY to your den, you sly old fox,
Your sins have found you out;
The farmer will leave his geese no more
While you are prowling about.

So for a dinner you must search
Within the forest dark,
Far from the farmer's deadly gun
And the watch-dog's fearful bark.

Your race is run if you he finds
Within his gates once more ;
He 'd put a bullet through your head
And nail it to the door.

For of his geese so fat and plump,
Full sixteen he has lost,

And if he lays his hands on you
You 'll have to pay the cost.

Now how much better, sly old fox,
It would have been for you,
If you had never learned to steal
His geese and chickens too.

By honest means if you had earned
Your food when you began,
You never would have cause to dread
The farmer and his gun.

--◆--

THE LARK.

FROM his humble grassy bed,
　　See the warbling lark arise !
By his grateful wishes led
　　Through those regions of the skies.

Songs of thanks and praise he pours,
　　Harmonizing airy space ;
Sings, and mounts, and higher soars,
　　Towards the throne of heavenly grace.

Small his gifts compared to mine,
　　Poor my thanks with his compared ;

I 've a soul almost divine ;
   Angels' blessings with me shared.

Wake, my soul ! to praise aspire ;
   Reason, every sense, accord ;
Join in pure seraphic fire ;
   Love, and thank, and praise the Lord !

———◆———

THE PALACE AND COTTAGE.

High on a mountain's haughty steep,
   Lord Hubert's palace stood ;
Before it rolled a river deep,
   Behind it waved a wood.

Low in an unfrequented vale
   A peasant built his cell,
Sweet flowers perfumed the cooling gale,
   And graced his garden well.

Loud riot through Lord Hubert's hall
   In noisy clamors rang ;
He scarcely closed his eyes at all,
   Till breaking day began.

In scenes of quiet and repose
   Young William's life was spent;
With morning's early beam he rose,
   And whistled as he went.

On sauces rich, and viands fine,
   Lord Hubert daily fed;
His goblet filled with sparkling wine,
   His board with dainties spread.

Warm from the sickle or the plough,
   His heart as light as air,
His garden ground, and dappled cow,
   Supplied young William's fare.

On beds of down beset with gold,
   With satin curtains drawn,
His feverish limbs Lord Hubert rolled,
   From midnight's gloom to morn.

Stretched on a hard and flocky bed,
   The cheerful rustic lay;
And sweetest slumbers lulled his head
   From eve to breaking day.

Fever, and gout, and aches, and pains,
   Destroyed Lord Hubert's rest;

Disorder burnt in all his veins,
   And sickened in his breast.

A stranger to the ills of wealth,
   Behind his rugged plough,
The cheek of William glowed with health
   And cheerful was his brow.

No gentle friend, to soothe his pain,
   Sat near Lord Hubert's bed ;
His friends and servants, light and vain,
   From scenes of sorrow fled.

But when on William's honest head
   Time scattered silver hairs,
His wife and children, round his bed,
   Partook and shared his cares.

The solemn hearse, the waving plume,
   A train of mourners grim,
Carried Lord Hubert to the tomb,
   But no one cared for him.

No weeping eye, no gentle breast,
   Lamented his decay,
Nor round his costly coffin pressed
   To gaze upon his clay.

But when upon his dying bed
   Old William came to lie;
When clammy sweats had chilled his head,
   And death had dimmed his eye;

Sweet tears, by fond affection dropped,
   From many an eyelid fell,
And many a lip, by anguish stopped
   Half spoke the sad farewell.

No marble pile, nor costly tomb,
   Describes where William sleeps;
But there wild thyme and cowslips bloom,
   And there affection weeps.

———◆———

THE GIPSY CAMP.

THE gipsy leads a merry life,
   When summer days are long,
With all his swarthy family,
   The leafy woods among.

No rent or taxes does he pay,
   His wants are few and small;
And round his fireside, blazing free,
   There's room enough for all.

Kind Nature for his shoeless feet
  A carpet green hath spread ;
With sunny skies and curtained clouds,
  For ceiling o'er his head.

When stormy winter strips the trees,
  The gipsy lodges then
In barn, or cave, or ruined tower
  Till summer comes again.

——◆——

THE SKYLARK.

HARK ! the Skylark's matin song
  Of his love and joy is telling,
With a pipe so clear and strong,
  All the feathered choir excelling.

In her nest his pretty mate,
  While he sings and soars above her,
With a throbbing breast elate,
  Listens to her tuneful lover.

Hark ! he bids the sluggard spring
  From a bed of sloth and dreaming,
And with grateful rapture sing,
  While the rosy morn is beaming.

Bird of love and bird of joy,
　Thou art thus a moral teacher,
From thy pulpit in the sky, —
　Temple of the tuneful preacher.

THE MASTER'S EYE.

Some little boys I've seen in school
　To learn so hard do try,
And bend so steady o'er their books
　Beneath the Master's eye.

But when 't is turned the other way,
　To learn they 're not inclined;
But play and laugh among themselves,
　Nor Master's rules do mind.

They little think how wrong it is
　Their Teacher thus to cheat,
Whose eye so kindly on them beams
　When in the school they meet.

Be honest with your teacher kind,
　To learn your lessons try;
When you 're unwatched as well as when
　Beneath the Master's eye.

MY MOTHER.

OF all the pretty words I know,
　Or ever yet have heard,
That sweetest from the lips can flow,
　" MY MOTHER " is the word.

Its gentle music most endears
　From childhood's guileless tongue,
But still its sound in riper years
　Can make the heart feel young ;

Can make it dream of childhood blest,
　And tears of gladness weep,
While pillowed on her gentle breast,
　And softly sung to sleep.

When pain or sickness bowed the head,
　And claimed her tender care,
13

A guardian angel o'er my bed
  My Mother still was there.

'T was she who taught my heart to pray,
  And trust in God above,
Through faith in the enduring stay
  Of Christ's Redeeming love.

THE TEN COMMANDMENTS.

To the one God who dwells above,
  Must I my worship give,
No other shall I fear or love,
  But he who bade me live.

His next command I must obey,
  And to no Idol kneel ;
No image either gold or clay,
  That does the earth reveal.

God's sacred name must I pronounce
  With reverence and with awe ;
A trifling tongue I will renounce,
  For fear I break his law.

And I must keep the Sabbath-day,
  Nor dare it to profane,

By useless work or foolish play
  To spend my time in vain.

To both my parents good and kind,
  All honor must I show,
Their just commands to bear in mind,
  And all their wishes know.

Foul murder next God doth forbid,
  By this his sacred law ;
Keep me, O Lord, from thought or deed,
  My soul doth much abhor.

From unclean words to keep our lips,
  His children he does tell,
To vice if I would turn my steps,
  I am forbid as well.

By thy command I must not steal,
  Not even a little pin ;
Thy words so wise they do reveal
  It is a grievous sin.

I must not lie, — it would be base
  To tell that which is wrong ;
With truthful lips and honest face,
  I 'll wend my way along.

To covet not my neighbor's store,
　His tenth command is given;
Let me his precepts study o'er,
　To fit myself for heaven.

———◆———

WE ARE SEVEN.

——— A SIMPLE child,
　That lightly draws its breath,
And feels its life in every limb,
　What should it know of death?

I met a little cottage girl,
　She was eight years old, she said;
Her hair was thick, with many a curl,
　That clustered round her head.

She had a rustic woodland air,
　And she was wildly clad;
Her eyes were fair, and very fair;
　Her beauty made me glad.

" Sisters and brothers, little maid,
　How many may you be? "
" How many?　Seven in all," she said,
　And wondrous looked at me.

" And where are they ? I pray you tell."
She answered, " Seven are we,
And two of us at Conway dwell,
  And two are gone to sea.

" Two of us in the churchyard lie,
  My sister and my brother,
And in the churchyard cottage, I
  Dwell near them with my mother."

" You say that two at Conway dwell,
  And two are gone to sea ;
Yet you are seven ! I pray you tell,
  Sweet maid, how this may be ? "

Then did the little maid reply,
  " Seven boys and girls are we,
Two of us in the churchyard lie,
  Beneath the churchyard tree."

" You run about, my little maid,
  Your limbs they are alive ;
If two are in the churchyard laid,
  Then you are only five ? "

" Their graves are green, they may be seen,"
  The little maid replied ;
" Twelve steps or more from mother's door,
  And they are side by side !

"My stockings there I often knit,
  My kerchief there I hem;
And there upon the ground I sit,
  And sing a song to them.

"And often, after sunset, sir,
  When it is light and fair,
I take my little porringer,
  And eat my supper there.

"The first that died was sister Jane,
  In bed she moaning lay;
Till God released her from her pain,
  And then she went away.

"So in the churchyard she was laid,
  And when the grass was dry,
Together round her grave we played,
  My brother John and I.

"And when the ground was white with snow,
  And I could run and slide,
My brother John was forced to go,
  And he lies by her side."

"How many are you, then," said I,
  "If they two are in heaven?"
Quick was the little maid's reply —
  "Oh, master, we are seven!"

" But they are dead — these two are dead,
Their spirits are in heaven!"
'T was throwing words away, for still
The little maid would have her will
And said, nay! we are seven.

OVER THE BROOK.

THE brook runs swift, my little Miss,
You ne'er could get across;
For stockings nice and tiny shoes
Would be a total loss.

But in your brother's sturdy arms
　　No danger you need fear,
He 'll safely cross to yonder bank
　　With little sister dear.

For well he loves his sister kind,
　　And tries to please her too ;
Would *all* the brothers that I know,
　　Were anxious so to do.

But some I know so rude are they,
　　Their sisters would not dare
To cross a brook within their arms,
　　Lest they should leave them there.

Brothers ! be to your sisters kind,
　　And help them all you can ;
For they will all your pains requite,
　　Before you are a man.

THE SCOTCH LADDIE.

COLD blows the north wind o'er the mountain
   so bare,
Poor Sawny benighted is travelling there;
His plaid-cloak around him he carefully binds,
And holds on his bonnet, that's blown by the
   winds.

Long time has he wandered his desolate way,
That wound him along by the banks of the
   Tay;

Now o'er this cold mountain poor Sawny must
    roam,
Before he arrives at his dear little home.

Barefooted he follows the path he must go,
The print of his footsteps he leaves in the snow :
And while the white sleet patters cold in his face,
He thinks of his home, and he quickens his pace.

But see, from afar he discovers a light,
That cheerfully gleams on the darkness of
    night,
And O what delights in his bosom arise !
He knows 't is his dear little home that he spies.

And now, when arrived at his father's own
    door,
His fears, his fatigues, his dangers are o'er ;
His brothers and sisters press round with de-
    light,
And welcome him in from the storms of the
    night.

For in vain from the north the keen winter
    winds blow ;
In vain are the mountain tops covered with snow ;
The snow of his country can never control
The affection that glows in the highlander's soul.

THE WATER-CRESS SELLER.

Now all aloud the wind and rain
Beat sharp upon the window-pane,
    And though 't is hardly light,
I hear that little girl go by,
Who does " fine water-cresses " cry,
    Morning, and noon, and night.

I saw her pass by yesterday,
The snow upon the pavement lay,
    Her hair was white with sleet;

She shook with cold, as she did cry,
" Fine water-cresses, come and buy,"
   And naked were her feet.

And with one hand, so red and cold,
She did her tattered bonnet hold,
   The other held her shawl,
Which was too thin to keep her warm,
But naked left each little arm,
   It was so very small.

Her water-cresses froze together,
Yet she, through the cold, bitter weather
   Went on from street to street ;
And thus she goes out every day,
For she can earn no other way
   The bread which she doth eat.

End.

CONTENTS.

208 CONTENTS.